Thomas Whit



# OUTLINES OF ROMAN LAW

CONSISTING CHIEFLY OF AN

ANALYSIS AND SUMMARY OF THE INSTITUTES

*FOR THE USE OF STUDENTS*

Elibron Classics
www.elibron.com

Elibron Classics series.



ISBN 1-4212-1355-9 (paperback)
ISBN 1-4212-1354-0 (hardcover)

This Elibron Classics Replica Edition is an unabridged facsimile of the edition published in 1872 by Stevens and Sons, London.

ENFRANCHISEMENT BY THE ROD.

P. 38.

# OUTLINES OF ROMAN LAW,

CONSISTING CHIEFLY OF AN

## ANALYSIS AND SUMMARY OF THE INSTITUTES.

*For the Use of Students.*

BY

T. WHITCOMBE GREENE, B.C.L.,

OF LINCOLN'S INN, BARRISTER-AT-LAW.

---

"The public reason of the Romans has been silently or studiously transfused into the domestic institutions of Europe, and the laws of Justinian still command the respect or obedience of independent nations."—*Gibbon.*

---

NEW EDITION.

LONDON:
STEVENS AND SONS,
119, CHANCERY LANE, FLEET STREET.
1872.

LONDON:

BRADBURY, EVANS, AND CO., PRINTERS, WHITEFRIARS.

# PREFACE.

The following Outlines form a new and enlarged edition of *An Analysis and Summary of the Institutes of Roman Law*. The work is based on the elementary treatises of Gaius and Justinian, and is intended to give in a concise form some insight into the great system of Roman jurisprudence. The important differences between the Institutes of Gaius and Justinian have been carefully noticed, quotations have been added from the Code and Digest, and frequent references will be found to Sir H. Maine's *Ancient Law* and to Austin's *Jurisprudence* (3rd edition). The Appendix contains extracts from the 44th chapter of Gibbon's *Roman Empire*, illustrating and explaining the subjects referred to in the text.

The creation of a new School of Law at Oxford, and the establishment of compulsory examinations for the English bar, cannot fail to promote the study of Civil Law in this country. The value and importance of the subject are continually becoming more generally appreciated.

An eminent judge * lately declared his want of sympathy with the attempt to introduce the study of English Law in the Universities. "English law was so practical, and such a mass of details, that little benefit could be obtained from studying it away from the courts. It was not a thing valuable as a mental training. As a means of education he preferred Roman law, which, more than any other system, exhibited the principles which ought to, and which did to some extent, underlie all the jurisprudence of all nations."

The author has to acknowledge the valuable assistance afforded by the works of Savigny, von Vangerow, Ortolan, Demangeat, Sandars, and other writers on the subject, and he hopes that the qualities of method and accuracy may be found in some measure to atone for the want of originality necessarily attaching to a legal abridgment.

* Lord Justice Mellish, at the Millenary Festival of University College, Oxford, June 12th, 1872.

LINCOLN'S INN,
*September*, 1872.

# CONTENTS.

# INTRODUCTION.

## THE HISTORICAL DEVELOPMENT OF ROMAN LAW.

FOUR periods have been assigned to the development of Roman Law. I. From the foundation of the City to the Law of the Twelve Tables, 750—450 B.C. Before the publication of the Twelve Tables, the traditional laws of Rome could only be ascertained by reference to habit and custom. In order to supersede so obscure and capricious a system, the diffusion of the art of writing suggested that a body of rules, solemnly approved by the people, should be inscribed on tablets and conspicuously exposed to the public view for common use and instruction. Accordingly a Commission of Decemvirs was appointed to execute this important work, and (probably with some assistance from the Laws of Solon) they completed the first ten tables in 450 B.C., the remaining two being added in the following year. From the fragments which exist of this early Code, it appears to have comprised rules affecting the most important rights and duties of the Roman citizen. But all that concerned the determination of the *dies fasti* and *nefasti*, the forms of procedure to be employed, and the interpretation of the law, remained the secret monopoly of the college of priests. *Omnium tamen harum et interpretandi scientia et actiones apud collegium Pontificum erant* (D. 1. 2. 2. 6). It was not till 150 years later that "the treachery of some plebeian officers at length revealed the profitable mystery." The Law of the Twelve Tables may be said to have lasted as long as the Roman people. Livy, writing in the time of Augustus, calls it *nunc quoque in hoc immenso aliarum super alias acervatarum legum cumulo fons omnis publici privatique juris* (III. 34). The prætors were employed in modifying its rules and supplying its deficiencies by importations from the Law of Nations (see p. 28 n.), and the jurists took it as the subject of their commentaries. Cicero says (De Legibus, II. 23) that the boys of his day used to learn it by heart as a "*carmen necessarium*," but that the practice had since been abandoned.

II. From the Law of the Twelve Tables to the birth of Cicero, 450—100 B.C., when *leges*, *plebiscita*, *senatus-consulta*, and *magistratuum edicta* were promulgated (see p. 30). In 366 B.C. the *prætor urbanus* was specially charged with the administration of justice. In 246 B.C. the first *prœtor peregrinus* was appointed. Fifty years later there were six prætors; Sulla raised the number to ten, and Julius Cæsar to twelve. Both the City and Foreign Prætors on entering office published Edicts declaring the principles by which their administration of the law would be governed. Nominally the authority of each edict lasted only for its framer's year of office, but its rules were probably always more or less adopted by his successor (*edictum tralatitium*). The Curule Ædiles, who had a considerable share of the administration of justice in connection with the sale of slaves and animals in the market, also published similar regulations. These edicts produced that *viva vox juris civilis*—the prætorian law. *Jus prœtorium est quod Prœtores introduxerunt, adjuvandi vel supplendi vel corrigendi juris civilis gratia, propter utilitatem publicam* (D. 1. 1. 7). "The prætor's edict," says Phillimore,* "with its rules and regulations, displays most conspicuously the extraordinary genius of the Romans for legislation. No method could be devised more effectually guarding against the

* "Private Law among the Romans," p. 54, &c. See also Austin, Lectures 28, 31, 32, and 40.

caprice of a magistrate on the one hand, and what Lord Bacon calls 'the froward retention of custom' on the other, than the scheme which obliged the judge before any case was brought before him to announce to the suitor the rule by which it would be determined." "The effect of this system was, that a supply of actual opinions and customs were added to the Roman Law, and that Roman jurisprudence kept pace with the exigencies of the age and the progress of society. The law was not a dead letter, but a living word."

The provinces were successively governed by special prætors, pro-prætors (having first held office as prætors at Rome), and pro-consuls, who issued provincial edicts, following as far as possible those of the two prætors in the city.

III. From the birth of Cicero to Alexander Severus, 100 B.C.—250 A.D., when the *edictum perpetuum*, the *principum placita*, and the *responsa prudentum*, were added to the formation of the law—"the learned and splendid age of jurisprudence." At the beginning of this period Servius Sulpicius* was the first to apply the Grecian philosophy to the reduction of general principles from particular cases: at the end of

* See an account of the earlier jurists by Pomponius (D. 1. 2. 2. 35-47).

the same period flourished the great jurists, Papinian,* Paul, Gaius, Ulpian, and Modestinus. "To these lawyers," says Austin (p. 568), "the Roman law owes the regularity and symmetry of its form, and the matchless consistency of its parts." In the time of Gaius the number of prætors at Rome had risen to eighteen, some of whom, as the *prætor fideicommissarius*, were charged with the conduct of special business. But the prætorian law had now been shaped from a confused and undigested mass into a regular and uniform system. In the reign of Hadrian, Salvius Julianus, an eminent prætor and jurist, was employed to collect and arrange the principles of the scattered edicts. This was called the *edictum perpetuum*, and although succeeding prætors still retained the legal power *jus edicendi*, they probably never departed from its rules. The *principum placita*, or Imperial constitutions, were either general or special, and consisted of *rescripta* or *epistolæ*, *decreta*, and *edicta*. Rescripts were written opinions on questions of law propounded by a public officer

* Papinian was the most celebrated of all the jurists. He was called the Asylum of Right and the Treasure of the Laws. In the time of Septimius Severus he held a prætorian court at York; some say with Paul and Ulpian (who were both his pupils) as his assessors. He died, probably by violence, at the age of 36. See pp. 9 and 13.

or a private person; *decreta* were judgments given on appeal, and *edicta* were general constitutions.* The *responsa prudentum* were the decisions and opinions of learned men empowered to interpret the law publicly. These jurisconsults were first authorised *in jure respondere* with imperial authority by Augustus, and from that time their opinions began to be sought as a privilege (*peti hoc pro beneficio cœpit* (D. 1. 2. 2. 47). It appears from Gaius (I. 7) that Hadrian sanctioned their authority *jura condere* by giving to their unanimous opinion the force of law, while he left questions on which they disagreed to the decision of the judge. As the prætors assisted, extended, and corrected the old civil law by their edicts, so the jurists supplied the deficiencies both of the civil and prætorian systems by their interpretations. This they effected in three ways—by writing books, by publishing *responsa*, and by discussion in the forum. The Digest affords evidence of their numerous writings. The *responsa* were given to clients who came to consult them, and also to *judices*. Their form was very short, and reasons were seldom added; but the jurists sometimes referred to the laws themselves, the authority of other *prudentes*, the practice of the forum, or the principles of

* See Austin, Lect. 28.

philosophy. When they disagreed on important and difficult questions, after consulting together and weighing their reasons, they came to a decision by a vote of the majority. This was called the *disputatio fori.** Hence many legal innovations were established which could be traced to no law or edict, but sprang solely from the minds of the jurists. Such were *acquisitio per arrogationem* (Inst. III. 10, pr.), codicils, the disinherison of posthumous children, the difference between the disinherison of sons and that of daughters and grandsons (p. 94), the Aquilian stipulation, the *regula Catoniana*, the exclusion of women beyond the degree of sisters from the succession of agnates (p. 127), the *actio rei uxoriæ*, and the complaint of the unnatural will. Although the principles arrived at by these discussions did not originally acquire at once the force of law, they were soon extended to similar cases by the practice of the forum and the addition of fresh authority. Hence arose the common terms *sententiæ receptæ*, *receptus mos*, *receptum jus*, *post multas variationes receptum*, and the *regulæ juris* were nothing but short statements of approved axioms and definitions. Justinian, in publishing the Digest, withdrew altogether the *facultas interpretandi*. The *responsa* bear a close resemblance to

* See Heineccius, *Antiquitates Romanæ*, p. 55.

English judge-made law, published through the medium of reported cases.

The frequent discussions of the jurists led to the formation of the two great schools of legal opinion founded respectively by Labeo and Capito. The Proculians, as the followers of the former were called, did not scruple to give a liberal and philosophical interpretation to the rules of the civil law when the changes of society required it, while the Sabinians, or disciples of Capito, persistently refused to depart from the strict letter of enactments once legally established.

IV. From Alexander Severus to Justinian, 250—550 A.D., when the whole power of legislation fell into the hands of the Emperors. "The period of jurists ends with Alexander Severus. From Hadrian to that emperor the improvement of the law was carried on, as it is at the present moment in most continental countries, partly by approved commentaries, and partly by direct legislation. But in the reign of Alexander Severus the power of growth in Roman Equity seems to be exhausted, and the succession of jurisconsults comes to a close. The remaining history of the Roman law is the history of the Imperial constitutions, and of attempts to codify what had now become the unwieldly body of

Roman jurisprudence."* The first attempt at codification was made by Gregorianus, a private lawyer, whose work contained Imperial constitutions, from Hadrian to Constantine the Great. The Code of Hermogenianus, also a private practitioner, consisted of a supplementary collection which is supposed to have been made in the reign of Constantine. Little is known of either, and their Codes included only special constitutions, or Rescripts. The works of the jurists, however, were the most important sources of the law, and these had been multiplied to such an extent that unless they could be reduced to a simple and harmonious system it was impossible that the decisions of the judges should have any steadiness or consistency. *Misera est servitus ubi jus aut incognitum est aut vagum.* Accordingly the famous constitution of Valentinian III. was published in A.D. 426, regulating their practical authority, originally in the Western Empire, but afterwards, by adoption into the Theodosian Code, also in the East. "All the works of the five jurists received the sanction of legal authority, with the exception of the notes of Ulpian and Paulus on Papinian. Only such doctrines of the other jurists received that sanction as were integrally contained and embodied in the works of

* Maine's *Ancient Law*, p. 68.

these five. When these jurists were not unanimous, the majority formed the rule; when they were equally divided, the opinion of Papinian was held as decisive; and in the event of his silence, the case was left to the determination of the judge."* In 438 Theodosius the younger published his Code, taking the collections of Gregorianus and Hermogenianus as his models. This work was contained in 16 books, and comprised both Edicts and Rescripts of 16 Emperors, beginning with Constantine, and extending over a period of 126 years. The compilers (eight in number) took nine years to complete their work, being empowered to eliminate superfluities, to make necessary additions, to alter ambiguities, and to correct inconsistencies. It established a uniform system of law for both the Eastern and Western Empires. "The Theodosian Code forms one of the most important monuments extant concerning the history of the law, whether we consider the great number of legislative enactments which it contains, or its application and influence upon the two divisions of the Roman world; an influence which in the Western Empire even survived its fall."† Theo-

* Savigny's *History of Roman Law*, c. 1.

† Ortolan's *History of Roman Law* (translated by Prichard and Nasmith), p. 42.

dosius also conceived the idea of forming a collection or Digest of the works of the jurists, but this was never carried into execution.

When the Empire of the West perished in A.D. 476, there existed, therefore, four practical sources of law—1, the works of the jurists, subject to the rule laid down in the Constitution of Valentinian III.; 2, the Gregorian and Hermogenian collections; 3, the Theodosian Code; and 4, the *Novellæ* or new and supplementary Constitutions of Theodosius.

"But the necessity of a second reform was urgent and general, and four different attempts were made to supply the defect within thirty years, each in a different kingdom, and independently of the others. 1. The Edict of the East Goth, Theodoric (A.D. 500). 2. The West Gothic (in Spain and the South of Gaul) Breviarium of Alaric II. (A.D. 506). 3. The Papian Law, among the Burgundians (soon after 500). 4. The Laws of Justinian, at first only for the Eastern Empire (528-534). The first of these is the rudest and worst of all, having modelled all the sources into a new system. The Papian is almost equally uninstructive, but gives some of the sources pure and unchanged."* The Breviarium of Alaric consists of, 1, a mutilated epitome of the

* Savigny's *History of Roman Law*, c. 1.

Institutes of Gaius, omitting altogether the fourth book; 2, an abridgment of the Received Opinions of Paul (5 books); 3, extracts from the Gregorian and Hermogenian Codes; and, 4, extracts from the Theodosian Code and *Novellæ*. Except the Epitome of Gaius, the texts are provided with a separate *scintilla* or interpretation.

The barbarous invaders of the West allowed their Roman subjects to preserve their separate manners and laws, and "from this state of society arose that condition of civil rights, denominated personal rights, or Personal laws, in opposition to Territorial laws." Hence it is said to have often happened that five men, each under a different law, might be found walking and sitting together. But as new nations were rapidly formed by amalgamation and intermarriages, the Roman law became interwoven with the customs of feudalism, the Personal laws surrendered to the Territorial, and the freedom and equality of the old communities were exchanged for the villeinage and subjection of military vassals. Still, in the South of France (the *pays de droit écrit*), and in the *cities* of Italy, the Roman law continued to flourish in its old exclusive form; whence, in later times, its doctrines spread their influence far and wide, and became the common source of European jurisprudence.

Justinian's legislation began with (1) the Code, published in A.D. 529, containing constitutions, both special and general, from the time of Hadrian. The Code was followed by (2) the Digest or Pandects,* in A.D. 534, which contain extracts, taken either directly or indirectly, from 39 jurists, and were intended to set forth the fundamental principles of the law. The main object of Justinian's plan was thus to abridge, in two separate works (1), the Imperial Constitutions and (2) the works of the Jurists, with a view to destroying all inconsistencies, uncertainties, and repetitions, and thus facilitating the use and popularizing the study of the law. *Nobis in legibus magis simplicitas quam difficultas placet.* It has been calculated that the extracts from Ulpian constitute about one-third of the work, from Paul about a sixth, and from Papinian about a twelfth. The Digest was accompanied by (3) the Institutes as a necessary work of introduction for the use of students (*cupida legum*

* The Digest is divided into seven parts and 50 books, each book having several titles, which are subdivided into laws, and these into paragraphs. Each title has also a heading or *principium.* The Code consists of 12 books. In the following pages the Code and Digest are quoted thus: C. or D. 3. 2. 1. *i.e.*, B. 3. T. 2. L. 1. Justinian's Institutes are sometimes quoted without special reference except at the head of each title.

*juventus*), arranged in a systematic or scientific method, according to distinctions lying in the subject-matter of the work. They are declared to be founded on all the old Institutional Treatises,* and especially on the Commentaries and *Res Quotidianæ* of Gaius, as well as many other Commentaries. They were compiled by Theophilus and Dorotheus under the superintendence of Tribonian. Finally (4), the Novels, or New Constitutions, effecting important changes, appeared shortly after Justinian's death. The *Corpus Juris Civilis* consists of these four works of Justinian.

In the East Justinian's Body of Law suffered little alteration for 300 years after his death, except that of abridgment and translation into other languages. In 886, Leo the Philosopher published a new body of laws called *Basilicæ*, which were improved and re-published by his son in 920. From that time the *Basilicæ*, with some new constitutions of succeeding emperors, continued to remain in force, till the capture of

* "The educational treatises, called Institutes or Commentaries, are among the most remarkable features of the Roman system. It was apparently in these Institutional works, and not in the books intended for trained lawyers, that the jurisconsults gave to the public their classifications and their proposals for modifying and improving the technical phraseology."—Maine's *Ancient Law*, p. 35.

Constantinople by the Turks in 1453 extinguished both the Eastern Empire and its laws.

In the fallen Western Empire Justinian's Law, with all its important reforms, was almost wholly unknown till the renewal of its study took place towards the close of the 11th century, the chief centre being the famous school of Bologna, which attracted students from all parts of Europe. In 1144, Vacarius the Lombard, coming from Bologna, founded a school of law at Oxford, where he introduced the Texts of Justinian with great success, having compiled an abridgment of the Code and Digest for the use of his pupils.*

* It is somewhat remarkable that while the degree of D.C.L. has remained the highest distinction which the University can bestow, and Bachelors of Civil Law still take precedence of Masters of Arts, the study of the subject should for a long period have been so conspicuously neglected at Oxford. In early times, though eagerly followed by the clergy, it obtained little favour from the laity, whose prejudices were aroused from the circumstance of its introduction from Italy, and the support it received from ecclesiastical authority. "Though the civil law," says Blackstone, "in matters of contract and the general commerce of life may be founded in principles of natural and universal justice, yet the arbitrary and despotic maxims which recommended it as a favourite to the Pope and the Romish clergy, rendered it deservedly odious to the people of England. *Quod principi placuit legis habet vigorem* (Inst. 1. 2. 6), the *magna charta* of the civil law, could never be reconciled with the *judicium parium vel lex terræ.*" Vol. I. p. 18, n. Stephen vainly attempted to forbid its study, and in the reign of Henry III. the clergy were excluded from practising in the secular courts. "But wherever they retired and wherever

In France, during the 12th and 13th centuries, the revived law of Justinian superseded that of Theodosius and Alaric in the *pays de droit écrit*, while in the Northern *pays de coutumes* it was treated as a scientific model and a necessary

their authority extended, they carried with them the same zeal to introduce the rules of the civil law, in exclusion of the municipal law. This appears in a particular manner from the spiritual courts of all denominations, from the Chancellors' Courts in both our Universities, and from the High Court of Chancery; in all of which the proceedings are to this day in a course much conformed to the civil law." On the other hand, the laymen who succeeded to the practice of the common law "entertained upon their parts a most hearty aversion to the civil law, and made no scruple to profess their contempt, nay, even their ignorance of it, in the most public way." *Ib.* p. 22. The settlement of the Common Pleas at Westminster, in the time of King John and Henry III., and the establishment of the Inns of Court as a juridical university in competition with Oxford and Cambridge, tended to foster the study of the municipal law to the detriment of that of the Roman jurisprudence. About the end of the 12th century, "the University of Oxford appears to have been distracted by the disputes of the students of law and of arts, the latter complaining that their faculty was neglected in favour of a science which only aimed at profit." In the reign of Edward II. these bickerings came to an open rupture, and on an appeal to the King a royal charter was ratified (afterwards confirmed by Richard II.), containing many privileges in favour of the faculty of Civil Law. At Cambridge, Henry V. found it necessary to command the students of Civil and Canon Law to attend the lectures of the professors, and to pay their fees. See Colquhoun's *Roman Civil Law*, vol. i., pp. 159, 275. "Formerly," says Fuller, "the Doctors of Canon Law preceded those of Civil Law, as the Pope makes himself to be above the Emperor. But King Henry VIII., stung with the dilatory pleas of the Canonists at branch of legal education. But it was not till the introduction of the Code Napoléon—the rules of which were borrowed largely from the Roman law, cleared of all feudal admixture—that a uniform system was established for the whole of France. Under the influence of French conquests, the diffusion of this modernized Roman jurisprudence over nearly the whole of Europe, even in countries where its acceptance might have been least expected, was rapid and permanent.

INSTITUTES OF GAIUS AND JUSTINIAN COMPARED.

Although the Commentaries of Gaius furnished the principal model for Justinian's Institutes, the two works will be found on comparison to present many striking points of difference. These arise partly from the nature and object of the treatises

Rome, in point of his marriage, did in revenge destroy their whole hive throughout his Universities, so that the Canon Law did never after stand by itself as a distinct faculty, but was annexed to Civil Law, and the degree denominated from the latter." *History of the University of Cambridge*, p. 167. The title of Bachelor and Doctor of *Laws* at Cambridge seems to have come into use in 1540—the date of the foundation of the Regius Professorship of Civil Law. The corresponding Chair at Oxford was founded in 1546. In the reign of Edward VI. it was represented to the King that the study of the Civil Law in both Universities was fast decaying, probably (Colquhoun thinks) from the diminution which the Reformation had caused in the revenues of the Church.

themselves, but chiefly from the continual progress of the law during the period of nearly four centuries which intervened between them, and particularly from the great changes of the imperial reformer. Little is known of the personal history of Gaius, except that he was the author of numerous legal works, and probably a teacher of law in the time of the Antonines. He was not one of the *prudentes quibus permissum est jura condere*, but the constitution of Valentinian III. ranks him among the other four great jurists with whom his name is generally associated, and his writings are frequently quoted in Justinian's Digest. His Commentaries are supposed to have been the first of the Institutional or elementary treatises, and he is said to have originated the famous division of law into Persons, Things, and Actions. The terseness of his style and the purity of his language contrast favourably with the more profuse sentences and the debased Latin of Justinian's compilers, who nevertheless followed closely his method and arrangement. It may be gathered from the general character of the Commentaries that they were intended for purposes of actual practice, while the Emperor's treatise, although declared to have the binding force of law, was primarily composed for academical instruction. It appears from a passage in his second book (II. 7) that Gaius was a provincial, and this may have led him to criticise as he does the peculiarities and exclusive doctrines of the pure Quiritary law. His Institutes (so remarkably recovered after lying hid for 1000 years) are evidently the work of a profound lawyer, conveying a clear and succinct account both of the jurisprudence of his own time and of those older institutions which had already passed away. It should be remembered in the present comparison that the Commentaries proceeded from the pen of Gaius alone, and were the first of the series of Introductory Treatises, while Justinian's Institutes were not only prepared by two authors under the superintendence of a third, but were also drawn from various independent sources. This will account for certain inconsistencies occurring in the latter, such as the distinction made in the first pages between the Law of Nations and the Law of Nature, but which disappears in the subsequent portion of the work. In many cases where the law remained unchanged Justinian's editors have adopted the very words of Gaius, in others they have given his meaning in different language, as in the following instance :—

| Gai. II. 189. | Just. I. 20. 26. |
|---|---|
| *Sed impuberes quidem in tutela esse omnium civitatium jure contingit, quia id naturali rationi conveniens est.* | *Impuberes autem in tutela esse naturali juri conveniens est.* |

Gaius gives no such definitions of law, jurisprudence, and other subjects, as may be found in Justinian, many of them being taken from the jurist Ulpian. The following subjects also (amongst others), noticed in Justinian's work, are not explained by Gaius:—*Peculium castrense*, and the general relations of father and son; *donationes*, servitudes, the unnatural will (*testamentum inofficiosum*), codicils, the degrees of relationship, the law of succession between mother and child (*SCC Tertullianum* and *Orphitianum*), the contracts of loan-for-use (*commodatum*), deposit and pledge, *quasi*-contracts and *quasi*-delicts, the revocation of legacies, preposterous stipulations, the divisions of mixed and civil and prætorian actions, *pauperies*, the office of *judex*, the subject of Criminal Law.

On the other hand, Gaius describes minutely many old institutions which had become entirely obsolete in Justinian's time, and are therefore subjects of peculiar interest. Such are the archaic forms of marriage (*confarreatio*, *coemptio*, and *usus*), *causæ probatio, manus* and *mancipii causa*, the perpetual tutelage of women, the ancient forms of transfer (*mancipatio* and *in jure cessio*), *usucapio pro herede, usureceptio, cretio, bonorum possessio sine re, emptio bonorum, sponsores, fidepromissores, adstipulatores, nomina transcriptitia, fictiones, præscriptiones pro actore, litis contestatio, furtum lance et licio conceptum.* He says little of *traditio* or delivery, which in Justinian's time had superseded *mancipatio* and *in jure cessio*. He refers on more than twenty occasions to the differences of opinion existing between the Sabinians and the Proculians, he himself being attached to the former school. In order to settle some of these disputed points, Justinian published his Fifty Decisions during the preparation of the Digest. Speaking of the Sabinians, he says, *hujusmodi scrupulositas nobis non placuit* (Inst. II. 20. 36). Gaius wrote under the formulary system of procedure which had disappeared 200 years before Justinian's legislation, and he explains very fully, not only the forms of pleading which were actually in use, but the old *legis actiones* which they had succeeded. These descriptions are the more valuable as neither of them are given in Justinian's Institutes. Gaius mentions the differences which had taken place in the will *per æs et libram* in his time, and describes the ceremony by which it was effected: Justinian gives the *testamentum tripartitum*, which, by an amalgamation of law and equity, superseded the mancipatory form. Gaius says that a slave instituted without simultaneous enfranchisement could not become the heir, even though subsequently manumitted: Justinian enacts that his enfranchisement shall always be implied in his institution. Gaius describes the old forms of legacies, and enumerates the differences existing in his time between them and *fideicommissa*, or bequests in trust: Justinian declares all legacies to be of the same nature, and reduces them to the level of *fideicommissa*. Gaius explains at great length and in various parts of his work, the condition of the *Latini Juniani* and *dedititii*: Justinian abolishes all difference between Roman citizens. Gaius carefully discriminates *res mancipi* and *res nec mancipi*: Justinian declares the distinction to be at an end. Gaius explains the various processes and results of interdicts: Justinian considers this superfluous, as they have been replaced by actions in the *judicia extraordinaria*. Justinian alters the law of manumission as prescribed in the *Leges Ælia Sentia* and *Furia*, and of emancipation; he modifies the power of acquisition through children under power by the invention of *peculium adventitium*, declaring the old right of parents to be *inhumanum* (II. 9. 1.); he alters the position of children adopted by an *extraneus* in regard to their rights of succession; he changes the law of usucapion and prescription; he extends to the provinces the law prohibiting the husband from selling or charging his wife's immovables, all difference between Italian and provincial soil being removed; he alters the law of *capitis deminutio, donationes, bonorum possessio*, disinherison, the succession between mother and children, novation, *satisdationes* in contracts and actions, *plus-petitio*, *furtum*, and *actio calumniæ;* he amalgamates the *SCC Trebellianum* and *Pegasianum;* he abolishes the *SC Claudianum*, also the rule mentioned by Gaius that the bequest of liberty made before the appointment of the heir is void, and the law prohibiting legacies to uncertain persons and *postumi alieni;* he reforms the law of succession between patrons and freedmen; he introduces *substitutio quasi-pupillaris;* he limits noxal actions to the cases of slaves and animals; he admits female agnates to equal rights of succession with males, affecting to restore the law of the Twelve Tables. These reforms prepared the way for the far more radical changes effected by the Novels. In the time of Gaius the civil and prætorian systems flourished in full vigour side by side, but it seems to have been the object of Justinian—particularly in his later legislation—

to overwhelm the old Quiritary law by large importations from the rules of equity, to substitute for a crude and ill-ordered *congeries* a reformed and simplified jurisprudence, and to complete that gradual change which he notices in the Institutes—*cum paulatim tam ex usu hominum quam ex constitutionum emendationibus, cœpit in unam consonantiam jus civile et prætorium jungi.* (II. 10. 3.)

## THE PERMANENT VALUE OF ROMAN LAW.

The following are some of the grounds on which the permanent value of the Roman law has been said to rest:*—1. Its great wealth in leading principles, and their logical application to daily life; the exactness of its terms, its symmetry, and close adherence to fundamental rules. 2. The scientific method and general literary excellence of the jurists. 3. From the comparative smallness of its volume, from its mastery of principles, their consistency (*elegantia*) and clearness of arrangement, there is no system of positive law which is so capable of being comprehensively grasped as a whole. 4. It illustrates in a remarkable manner the general history of law, and is valuable for purposes of contrast and compari-

* See Savigny's *Modern Roman Law; Cambridge Essays*, 1856, pp. 1—29; and Austin's *Jurisprudence*, p. 1114.

son.* 5. It is the key to international law, to the civil law of nearly all Europe and of a large part of America. Even in England, much of the Ecclesiastical Law and Equity, and some portion of the Common Law (particularly the mercantile), is derived from the Roman, either immediately or through the Canon Law. 6. It affords a model of legal thought and principles to which English law is steadily and inevitably tending.† 7. It is the solvent of feudal custom and barbarous usage. 8. It furnishes valuable instruction in the interpretation and application of express written rules. 9. It is rapidly becoming the *lingua franca* of universal jurisprudence and diplomacy. 10. It is a most important element in the general mass

* See *Ancient Law*, p. 24.

† It is sufficiently obvious that our own legal system is still lingering in a condition corresponding to those intermediate stages through which the Roman law passed in advancing towards its simplification and maturity. But it is difficult to suppose that English law can long remain unaltered in respect either of its form or substance, its judicature or procedure. Schemes for the collection and arrangement of its multitudinous and scattered fragments have been frequently suggested; the law of primogeniture, the distinction between real and personal property, copyhold tenure and other remnants of feudalism have been threatened with abolition; the fusion of law and equity, a re-arrangement of our tribunals, a further simplification of the forms of pleading, the pruning away of legal fictions, a modification of the present system of juries, are among the changes constantly urged by reformers in the direction of uniformity and in the interests of justice.

of human knowledge. 11. Although an acquaintance with Roman law may not be necessary to ensure success as a practitioner, it is almost indispensable for the judge, the jurist, the diplomatist, and the draftsman. 12. It is a collection of the rational opinions and accumulated experience of the wisest lawyers and the ablest intellects of the world, which may be referred to as a scientific—although not binding—authority, when the municipal laws are silent or obscure. *Servatur ubique jus Romanum non ratione imperii, sed imperio rationis.*

# OUTLINES OF ROMAN LAW.

## OF JUS, OR LAW.

Inst. I. 1. 2. Gai. I. 1—8.

*Justitia* is the constant and perpetual wish to render to everyone his right (*jus suum*).

*Jurisprudentia* is the knowledge of things divine and human; the science of right and wrong.

*Juris præcepta*, the maxims of law, are to live *honeste* (morally, virtuously), to hurt no one, to give everyone his due.*

*Jus*, or Law, is, I. *Publicum*; II. *Privatum*.

I. *Jus publicum* regards the constitution and government of the Roman Empire.

II. *Jus privatum* determines the mutual rights and obligations of individuals. It consists of pre-

* These maxims appear to confound law and morality. *Non omne quod licet honestum est* (D. 50. 17. 144), for the moral rules belong chiefly to the *forum conscientiæ*. But *jus* is probably used here in an extended sense.

cepts of, 1, *jus naturale;* 2, *jus gentium;* and 3, *jus civile.* (Justinian here follows the division of Ulpian.)

1. *Jus naturale* is the immutable law which Nature teaches both men and animals.

2. *Jus gentium* is the law of reason which is held good uniformly among all nations.*

* "As intercourse between the Roman people and foreign nations increased, it became necessary to know and to apply the law of other states in the administration of Roman justice. The wider the Roman dominion spread, the wider became the views of their jurists, and in this way arose the notion of a law common to the Romans with other nations, and with all mankind." (Phillimore's *Roman Law*, p. 24.)

Sir H. Maine condemns Ulpian's lawyer-like attempt to distinguish between the *jus naturale* and the *jus gentium.* "The difference between them is entirely historical, and no distinction in essence could ever be established. The *jus gentium* was a collection of rules and principles determined by observation to be common to the institutions which prevailed among the various Italian tribes. The *jus naturale* is simply the *jus gentium* seen in the light of a peculiar theory. . . . It is notorious that this proposition—live according to Nature—was the sum of the tenets of the famous Stoic philosophy. Now, in the subjugation of Greece, that philosophy made instantaneous progress in Roman society. . . . The alliance of the Roman lawyers with the Stoic philosophers lasted through many centuries. . . . After Nature (a term implying symmetrical order both in the moral and physical world) had become a household word in the mouths of the Romans, the belief gradually prevailed among the Roman lawyers that the *jus gentium* was, in fact, the lost code of Nature, and that the Prætor in framing an Edictal jurisprudence on the principles of the *jus gentium* was gradually restoring a type from which law had only departed to deteriorate. . . . The ideas of simplification and

3. *Jus civile* is the municipal law of a particular State, as of Athens or of Rome. It is liable to frequent changes.

*E.g.*, "The law of nature instructs most animals to cherish and educate their infant progeny. The law of reason inculcates to the human species the returns of filial piety. But the exclusive, absolute and perpetual dominion of the father over his children is peculiar to the Roman jurisprudence." (Gibbon, c. 44).

Gaius includes the *jus naturale* in the *jus gentium*, as the law of natural reason common to all mankind, and Justinian afterwards adopts this division: "All nations who are ruled by laws and customs, use partly their own particular laws and partly those which are common to all mankind. The law which a people enacts for itself is called

generalisation had always been associated with the conception of Nature; simplicity, symmetry, and intelligibility came therefore to be regarded as the characteristics of a good legal system, and the taste for involved language, multiplied ceremonials and useless difficulties disappeared altogether. The strong will and unusual opportunities of Justinian were needed to bring the Roman law to its existing shape, but the ground-plan of the system had been sketched long before the imperial reforms were effected." *Ancient Law*, c. 3. Savigny thinks Ulpian merely meant to say that the relation of the sexes and the propagation and nurture of offspring are common to all animals. He did not intend to ascribe law to animals which are not human, but only the natural relation, which is the foundation of law.

the Civil Law of that people, but that which natural reason appoints for all mankind is called the Law of Nations, because all nations use it." (Inst. I. 2, and Gai. I. 1).

*Jus civile* is, I. *Scriptum;* and II. *Non scriptum.*

I. *Jus scriptum* consists of, 1, *leges*, or enactments by the whole body of the Roman people, proposed by a senatorial magistrate;* 2, *plebiscita*, enactments by the *plebs* or citizens not being senators or patricians;† 3, *senatus-consulta*, decrees of the senate; 4, *principum placita*, decrees of the emperors (*rescripta* or *epistolæ, decreta, edicta*), also called "*constitutiones;*" 5, *magistratuum edicta*, edicts of the prætors or curule ædiles, forming the "*jus honorarium;*" 6, *responsa prudentum*, the decisions and opinions of learned persons authorised to interpret the law publicly. (See Introduction, p. 6, and *Ancient Law*, p. 33.)

II. *Jus non scriptum* is the unwritten law established by ancient custom, *ut apud Græcos: τῶν νόμων οἱ μὲν ἔγγραφοι οἱ δὲ ἄγραφοι. Diuturni mores consensu utentium comprobati legem imitantur.* (Inst. I. 2. 9.) In order to acquire greater cer-

* *Lex aut rogatur, id est, fertur: aut abrogatur, id est, prior lex tollitur: aut derogatur, id est, pars primæ legis tollitur: aut subrogatur, id est, adjicitur aliquid primæ legi: aut obrogatur, id est, mutatur aliquid ex prima lege.* (Ulpian, *Regulæ*, I. 3.)

† By the *Lex Hortensia*, B.C. 286, *plebiscita* were declared to bind the whole *populus* including patricians. Gai. I. 3.

tainty the rules of custom often pass from Unwritten into Written law. Gaius does not give this division.

*Jus privatum* relates, I. to Persons; II. to Things; III. to Actions.

See Austin, *Lectures* 28, 31, 32, 40; also Maine's *Ancient Law*, c. 3.

# BOOK I.—OF PERSONS.

## OF FREE MEN AND SLAVES.

Inst. I. 3—7. Gai. I. 9—47, 52—54, 65—86, III. 56—76.

*Persona* (literally an actor's mask) is used to mean (1) a human being, (2) a *status* or condition borne by a man (*unus homo sustinet plures personas*), and (3) a man invested with rights or subject to obligations.*

All men are either, 1, free (*ingenui, libertini*); or 2, slaves (*servi, mancipia, vernæ*). *Summa divisio de jure personarum hæc est, quod omnes homines aut liberi sunt aut servi.*†

Freedom is the natural power of doing anything we please that is not prohibited by force or law. Slavery is an institution of the *jus gentium*, by

* Austin disputes the last definition, attributing it partly to a confusion of the two first significations. *Lect.* 12, p. 363.

† Since slaves could be dealt with as articles of property (Inst. II. 2), they would appear in some respects to belong rather to the division of Things. But their capacity to take part in a legal transaction, *e.g.* as purchasers or legatees, entitles them to rank among Persons. *Servi persona inspicitur in testamentis.* (Paul, D. 31. 82. 2.)

which, contrary to natural right,* one man becomes the property of another.

Free persons are (1) *cives ex jure Quiritium*, or pure Roman citizens, and (2) *peregrini*, or foreigners.† They are also (3) *ingenui*, and (4) *libertini*.

* This illustrates the double meaning of *jus naturale*. "The law of Nature, or *jus gentium*, which authorised slavery, and that which repugns it, cannot be the same. It sometimes means that portion of positive law which is a constituent part of all positive systems, and sometimes the standard to which, in the opinion of the writer, law should conform." Austin, *Lect.* 31, p. 583.

† An important distinction long existed at Roman law between *cives* and *peregrini*, for citizens *ex jure Quiritium* enjoyed public and private rights, which were persistently denied to the members of other states, whether subjects of Rome or independent. These were designated—first, as *hostes*, then *peregrini*, and finally, *provinciales*. When conquered, they were allowed for the most part to preserve their own particular laws and customs. The principal rights of the *civis* consisted of the *jura*, (1) *suffragii et honorum* (voting and public offices), (2) *commercii* (capacity to enter into the solemn forms of conveyance, &c.), and (3) *connubii* (capacity to contract Quiritary marriage). But as the relations between Rome and foreign communities increased, it became necessary to modify the exclusiveness of the *civitas*. The *Jus Latii* extended private rights to the *Latini*, the *Jus Italicum* gave privileges to towns and territories, and the *municipes*, or burgesses of independent *municipia*, were placed in the enjoyment of the *commercium* and the *connubium*. In addition to these concessions, a special *prætor peregrinus* was appointed in 246 B.C. to determine civil cases in Italy, (1) between *cives* and members of dependent states; (2) between members of one such state and those of another; (3) between members of subject states living in Rome. The body of subsidiary law introduced by the edicts of these

An *ingenuus* is one who is free from his birth, being born in lawful matrimony of parents both

prætors, and administered by them, was known as the *jus gentium* of the earlier Romans, that is to say, a collection of rules common to, or conversant about, those *gentes* who were subjects of the Roman people. "After the dominion of Rome" (says Austin, p. 576) "had extended beyond Italy, the same or a similar law was administered in the outlying provinces (by their own respective Presidents or Governors) in aid of the law peculiar to Rome herself, or of the law obtaining in any of those provinces before its subjection to the conquering city." It therefore became nearly uniform throughout the whole Roman empire. This *jus gentium* "was the only *jus gentium* that was known to the Roman law, till the *jus gentium* or *naturale*, which occurs in Justinian's compilations, was imported into it by the jurists, who are styled Classical, from speculations of Greek Philosophers on Law and Morals." Austin proceeds to show that the *jus gentium* having first arisen in an age comparatively enlightened, and being a product of large experience, was gradually incorporated with the *jus civile*, which had arisen in an age comparatively barbarous, and was a product of narrow experience. This was accomplished partly by acts of the Populus, Plebs, and Senate, and by opinions of the *Prudentes*, but principally through the edicts of the *Prætores Urbani*, most of which were formed on the model of the *jus gentium*. "So much, indeed, of the *jus gentium* passed into the *jus prætorium*, that one of the names given to the latter was probably transferred to it from the former. It probably was named *æquitas* (or *jus æquum*) after that *æqual* or *common* law, from which it had borrowed the bulk, or a large portion, of its provisions." (*Lect.* 31). Sir H. Maine, however, thinks "that the word was at first a mere description of that constant *levelling* or removal of irregularities which went on wherever the prætorian system was applied to the case of foreign litigants." (*Anc. Law* p. 60.) The Emperors distributed largely the *jus civitatis*, particularly Trajan and Hadrian: Caracalla extended it to all the free subjects of the empire, and finally Justinian bestowed it upon all *libertini*.

born free, or both made free, or one of whom has been born and the other made free, or whose mother is free at the time of conception, pregnancy, or birth, though the father be a slave. But see *SC Claudianum* (p. 142).

*Libertini*, or freedmen, are those who have been manumitted from lawful slavery. They were originally in one, and afterwards in three classes: 1, complete *liberti*, full Roman citizens; 2, less complete, or *Latini Juniani*, with *commercium*, but without *connubium* or *suffragium*; 3, in the scale of *dedititii*, or people conquered in war. The *dedititii*, though personally free, had no political rights (not even *commercium*). They were forbidden to live within a 100 miles of Rome, and were incapable of ever becoming Roman citizens.

Gaius explains fully the condition of *Latini* and *dedititii*. Slaves who had been put in chains, branded, found guilty of an offence after examination by torture, or consigned to the amphitheatre or prison, and who were afterwards manumitted, were in the scale of *dedititii*. If not so disgraced, a slave became a *Latinus* by enfranchisement, unless (1) he was over thirty years, (2) he belonged to his master *ex jure Quiritium*, and (3) he was enfranchised *justâ ac legitima manumissione*, *i.e.*, by the *vindicta*, *census*,

D 2

or will. If these three conditions were fulfilled, he became a full Roman citizen.

The *Latini* were so called because they stood on a footing with the Latin colonists, and *Juniani* because they received their liberty under the *Lex Junia Norbana* (A. U. C. 671). *Admonendi sumus eos qui nunc Latini Juniani dicuntur olim ex jure Quiritium servos fuisse, sed auxilio prætoris in libertatis forma servari solitos* (Gai. III. 56). The *Lex Ælia Sentia* (A.D. 4) denied them the *testamenti factio* (p. 93), but they could take by *fideicommissum* (p. 116). They had no *patria potestas*. But *Latini* could become Roman citizens by (1) *iteratio*, a second manumission fulfilling the above three conditions; (2) *causæ probatio*, if, in the case of a union between a *Latinus* and a *civis Romana* or a *Latina*, a child was born who reached the age of one year (*anniculus*), the prætor after solemn proof could order father, mother, and son (if born a *Latinus*) to take the rank of citizens; (3) *erroris causæ probatio*, if a Roman citizen married unwittingly (*per ignorantiam*) one who had not the *connubium*, the cause of error might be justified, and the want of citizenship would be supplied; (4) a *Latina* giving birth to three children; (5) imperial grant; (6) military service (at first six years, afterwards three); (7) ship-building, and carrying wheat to Rome for six years; (8) *ædificio et pistrino*, by building a house, or establishing a mill or bakehouse.

Justinian abolishes all distinctions between *liberti*, and (in the 78th Novel) between *libertini* and *ingenui*, reserving only the rights of the patron when they were not renounced.

Slaves are, 1, born so (*vernæ*), when their mother is a slave during the whole time of her pregnancy, for such children follow the condition of their mother (*partus sequitur ventrem*); 2, they become so by the law of nations by captivity in war (*mancipia*), or under the civil law, by (1) failing to perform military service, (2) non-registration in the *census*, (3) by *addictio* for debt (these causes belonged to the older law); by (4) the voluntary sale of a free man above twenty years of age, (5) the cohabitation of a free woman with a slave (p. 142), (6) ingratitude on the part of a freedman, (7) the condemnation of a free man to the mines or amphitheatre, *servus pœnæ*, or *servus sine domino* (abolished in the Novels). Slaves can have no proprietary rights, and whatever they acquire is gained for their masters, who may allow them to retain a *peculium*, or small patrimony.

Manumission is the gift of liberty to a slave. A master who has manumitted a slave becomes his patron.

*The modes of manumission.* Under the solemn forms of the older law: 1, by the *vindicta, i.e.*, a fictitious suit in which the *assertor libertatis* declared the slave's freedom before the prætor, and touched him with a wand (*vindicta*);* 2, by will,

* The accompanying representation of the *manumissio per vindictam* is taken from an ancient marble at Rome. J. F. Christius, in his *Noctes Hallenses*, gives the following explanation: *Duo videlicit apparent in hac imagine servuli, pileati, nudi cætera, nisi quod inguen linteo tecti: alter, puto, jam manumissus, manu autem mittendus alter. Is quidem ad pedes patroni provolutus, pro data libertate gratias agit. Sic enim servi consueerant etiam deprecari. Alterius vero servi currentis et scuticam læva tenentis, qua uti solebant, opinor, ad submovendam in publico turbam obvium, sibique festinantibus subinde molestam, herus dextram prehendit, quod manumissionis signum erat. Nil ergo restat in hoc lapide e manumittentis simulacro, præter dextram ejus servo porrectam, cætera vetustate confracta sunt. Adstat prætor togatus, prolixo atque fluctuante, quod elegantiæ fuerat, sinu: dextrâ gestans virgam seu bacillum, ex more nimirum magistratuam. Lævâ vero prætor tractat vindictam, seu festucam: quâ deinde lictori traditâ, servus e manu domini missus circumagebatur.* The *festuca*, or *vindicta*, represents the weapon of the Roman foot soldier. *Festucâ utebantur, quasi hastæ loco, signo quodam justi dominii, quia maxime sua esse credebant qua ex hostibus cepissent.* (Gai. IV. 16.) As the process was fictitious, it was not necessary for the magistrate to be holding his tribunal. *Non est omnino necesse pro tribunali manumittere: itaque plerumque in transitu servi manumitti solent, cum aut lavandi, aut gestandi, aut ludorum gratiâ prodierit Prætor aut Proconsul Legatusve Cæsaris.* (Gai. D. 40. 2. 5.) Cf. Gai. I. 20. Ulpian allowed the presence of the lictor to be dispensed with. *Ego, cum in villa cum Prætore fuissem, passus sum apud eum manumitti, etsi lictoris præsentia non esset.* (D. 40. 2. 8.) Hermogenianus says that the solemn words, *licet non dicantur, ut dicta accipiuntur.* (Ib. L. 23.)

when the freed slave is called "*orcinus:*" if conditionally free, "*statu liber;*" 3, by enrolling the slave's name in the *census*. Under the later law: 4, before the bishops of the church; 5, in the presence of friends; 6, by letter; 7, by any testamentary paper or codicil; 8, by many other ways introduced by the emperors. The forms of enfranchisement by the *vindicta* and by will (but not by the *census*) remained in force in Justinian's time.

*Restraints on manumission.* By the *Lex Ælia Sentia* it was void if made *in fraudem creditorum vel in fraudem patroni.** By the same law, a master under twenty could only manumit by the *vindicta*, upon some lawful ground approved by the council.† But Justinian allows a master after seventeen to manumit by will, and repeals the *Lex Furia Caninia* (8 A.D.), which limited such manumission as follows: the owner of two slaves could enfranchise both; of three, two; of from four to ten, half; of from ten to thirty, a

* Gaius mentions that the provision against defrauding creditors by manumission was the only part of the Lex that applied to *peregrini*. (I. 47.)

† The council consisted, at Rome, of five Senators and five knights; in the provinces, of twenty Roman citizens, call l *Recuperatores*. Lawful cause of manumission would be the case of a near relation, a *pædagogus*, a *servus procuratoris habendi gratiâ*, or an *ancilla matrimonii causâ*. (Gai. I. 19. 20. 39.)

third, but always at least five; of from thirty to one hundred, a fourth, but at least ten; of from one hundred to five hundred, a fifth, but at least twenty-five; but never more than one hundred. Each slave was to be individually named in the will. There were no restrictions on manumission *inter vivos.*

After manumission the mutual duty of support, in case of poverty, remains to the patron and freedman, and if the freedman dies intestate, without children, the patron succeeds. (See p. 132.)

The power of a master over his slaves is called *dominica potestas.* This *potestas* was almost unlimited down to the time of the Antonines, when extreme punishments were forbidden. (Gai. I. 52. 53). In the time of Sulla the intentional murder of another man's slave was made punishable with exile and death. Antonine extended this to the case of a man's own slave. He also provided that a slave who was badly treated might demand to be sold. The *Lex Petronia* (*temp.* Augustus) forbade the condemnation of slaves to fight with wild beasts. Hadrian required the sanction of a magistrate for their death, and Constantine permitted only moderate corporal chastisement. Seneca says, *in servo nihil domino non licet*, but Justinian observes, *expedit reipublicæ ne quis suâ re malè utatur.*

The master who owns the slave *in bonis* (Gai. II. 40—42) has the *potestas: nam qui nudum jus Quiritium in servo habet, is potestatem habere non intelligitur.* (Gai. I. 54.)

### OF THE PATERNAL POWER (*Patria potestas*).

Inst. I. 8. 9. Gai. I. 55—57, 87, 88, 93, 94; II. 87.

Persons are, I. Independent (*sui juris*); and II. Subject to another's power (*alieni juris*).

*Familia* is used to signify (1) the master of a house and all who are subject to his authority, his wife, children, and slaves; (2) the *agnati* or relations through *males* (see p. 58), who make up the *familia civilis;* (3) the *cognati*, or all blood relations; (4) anciently, a person's *patrimonium* and *sacra privata* (*e.g.*, *actio familiæ erciscundæ*, p. 73); and (5) the slaves of a household.

In a *familia*, the *paterfamilias* alone is *sui juris;* the rest are all *alieni juris*, being subject to his power.

*Extent of a father's power.* Over his children born in lawful matrimony, or any descendants sprung from his son, but not from his daughter; also over children or descendants gained by adoption. A child born of a man's daughter is in the power of its own father. A woman can have no descendants in her power. Ulpian says, *Mulier familiæ suæ et caput et finis est.* "A female name closes the branch or twig of the genealogy in which it occurs. . . . If a woman died unmarried, she could have no legitimate descendants. If she married, her children fell under the *patria potestas*, not of her father, but of her husband, and were thus lost to her own family." (*Anc. Law*, pp. 148, 149.)

*Patria potestas*, like *dominica potestas* consisted of, 1, *jus acquirendi per;* 2, *jus venumdandi*, or the power of sale; and 3, *jus vitæ et necis*, the jurisdiction of life and death. This power was gradually reduced by the emperors. Trajan deprived a cruel father of his *patria potestas.* Alexander Severus created superintendents to protect children. Diocletian forbade their sale, and Constantine made the murder of a son punishable as parricide.

*How acquired.* 1. By lawful marriage. 2. By legitimation. 3. By adoption.

*How ended.* 1. By the death of father or child. 2. By father or child suffering loss of freedom or citizenship (but not by a temporary *relegatio in insulam*). 3. By the child attaining civil or religious dignities. 4. By emancipation (see p. 53). 5. By mutual consent of father and child. 6. By the father suffering *arrogatio.*

7. By the child's adoption into another family.
8. By a daughter's marriage involving *conventio in manum viri.* If the father is taken prisoner, his power is suspended during captivity, but revives on returning by the *jus postliminii*—the law which restores retaken property to its owners and returned prisoners to their rights. *Duæ sunt species postliminii, aut ut ipsi revertamur, aut ut aliquid recipiamus.* (Heineccius.)

"The Family, as held together by the *Patria Potestas*, is the *nidus* out of which the entire Law of Persons has germinated. (Maine, p. 152.)

The *patria potestas* is peculiar to the Romans, but was also known to the Galatians (see St. Paul's Epistle to the Galatians, iv. 1—3).

The *dominica potestas* was an institution of the *jus gentium.*

See Appendix, p. 205; and *Ancient Law*, pp. 122—146, where Sir H. Maine compares the social condition of the Hebrew Patriarchs.

## OF MARRIAGE.

### Inst. I. 10. Gai. I. 56—91, 108—115.

*Nuptiæ sive matrimonium est viri et mulieris conjunctio, individuam vitæ consuetudinem continens.*

*Matrimonium* is, 1, *justum* or legally contracted; and 2, *non justum*.

The old forms of marriage by which the wife passed *in manum viri*, and stood in the position of daughter to her husband, being subjected to his *patria potestas*,* were: 1, *confarreatio*, a religious ceremony in which the parties, "seated on the same sheep-skin, tasted a salt cake of *far*, or rice;" 2. *coemptio*, a fictitious sale, *per æs et libram*, of the wife to the husband; 3, *usus*, or cohabitation for a whole year, with intention of marriage. For an account of these forms, see Gai. I. 110—115. Ulpian says: *Farre convenit uxor in manum, certis verbis, et testibus decem præsentibus, et sollenni sacrificio facto, in quo panis quoque farreus adhibetur.* (*Regulæ*, IX. 1.) *Coemptio* is sup-

* Livy calls this *servitus muliebris*, xxxiv. 7. *Manus* is analogous to *patria potestas*, but *in potestate quidem et masculi et feminæ esse solent, in manum autem feminæ tantum conveniunt.* (Gai. I. 109.) *Manus, adoptio, servitus, patronatus, mancipii causa, tutela,* and *curatio* were the means by which the Romans fictitiously or artificially extended the natural relations of the family.

posed to have been an accessory ceremony to *confarreatio.* In Cicero's time it seems to have generally superseded the latter, in consequence, probably, of the growing indifference to the old ceremonies, the difficulty and expense attending them, and the increasing freedom of divorce. In *usus*, the usucapion was interrupted and the *conventio in manum* delayed by the wife absenting herself from her husband for three nights in the year. Gaius says that this form was abolished in his time, partly by legislation and partly by disuse. A woman married without any of these ceremonies was called *matrona* instead of *materfamilias.*

At this stage of Roman law all the wife's property passed absolutely to the husband, and if she survived him she was subject to the guardian whom he might appoint by will. *Quidquid adquirebat uxor, marito adquirebat, omnia enim quæ ejus erant viri fiebant dotis nomine.* Husbands had the power of life and death over wives *in manu*, as well as that of sale.

As *conventio in manum* gradually disappeared,*

* "At the most splendid period of Roman greatness, the fashion of wedlock amounted to little more than a temporary deposit of the woman by her family. The rights of the family remained unimpaired, and the lady continued in the tutelage of guardians whom her parents had appointed, and whose privileges of control overrode, in many material respects, the inferior authority of her husband."—*Ancient Law*, p. 156.

the mere consent of the parties formed the legal contract, with or without writing. *Nuptias, non concubitus, sed consensus facit.*

*Conditions of lawful marriage.* 1. The male must be fourteen years of age (puberty), and the female twelve (*nubilis*, of marriageable age). 2. Consent of the parties, and in some cases of their parents. 3. *Connubium*, or legal capacity to contract Quiritary marriage. *Connubium habent cives Romani cum civibus Romanis; cum Latinis autem et peregrinis ita, si concessum est.* (Ulpian, *Regulæ*, V. 2.) 4. The parties must be previously unmarried, and not within prohibited degrees of relationship. See below.

*Impediments to justum matrimonium.* 1. Direct relationship between ascendants and descendants in any degree, by blood or adoption. 2. Collateral relationship, when either person is in the first degree from the common ancestor. The degree of collateral relationship of any two persons is calculated by adding together the sum of their respective steps of descent from their common ancestor. *E. g.*, first cousins are in the fourth degree, and may legally marry. 3. Affinity, or relationship between each married person and the ascendants or descendants of the other. *E. g.*, a man may not marry his step-mother or step-daughter, his mother-in-law or daughter-in-law:

but he may marry the daughter of his step-mother by a previous marriage. The Christian emperors forbade marriage between son-in-law and daughter-in-law. There can be no degrees in affinity. 4. Natural defects of mind or body. 5. Marriage is prohibited between the governor of a province and a native; 6, between guardian and ward; 7, between senators and *liberti;* 8, between Jews and Christians; 9, between tutor, or curator, or their son or grandson, and a pupil under twenty-six; 10. In 415 A.D. Theodosius II., confirming a previous edict of Constantius II. in 355, declared marriage with a deceased wife's sister to be incestuous and the issue illegitimate.

Children born in lawful matrimony follow the condition of the father, and their rights date from the time of conception. Otherwise they follow the condition of the mother, and their rights date from the time of birth.

*How dissolved. Dirimitur matrimonium divortio,* morte, captivitate, vel alia contingente ser-*

* After the first six centuries from the foundation of the city, divorces became frequent at Rome. Wives were discarded not only for immorality, old age, and sterility, but for such slight reasons as going out of doors without a head-dress, secretly conversing with a common freedwoman, or attending the public games without their husbands' knowledge. Plutarch says that Cicero divorced Terentia in order to pay off a debt with a new dowry; and Publilia, because she showed signs of joy at the

*vitute utrius eorum.* (D. 24. 2. 1.) Marriage effected by *confarreatio* or *coemptio* was dissolved by *diffarreatio* and *remancipatio.*

The *libellus repudii* is a written message, announcing the divorce, sent by the hand of a freedman in the presence of seven Roman citizens of full age. Theodosius II. and Valentinian made this an essential condition of divorce (C. 5. 17. 8 pr.). *Nullum divortium ratum est nisi septem civibus Romanis puberibus adhibitis, præter libertum ejus qui divortium faciet.* (D. 24. 2. 9.) *Inter divortium et repudium hoc interest, quod repudiari etiam futurum matrimonium potest: non recte autem sponsa divortisse dicitur: quod divortium ex eo dictum est, quod in diversas partes eunt, qui discedunt.* (Paul, D. 50. 16. 191.) *In repudiis autem, id est, renunciatione, comprobata sunt hæc verba:* TUAS RES TIBI HABETO. (Gai. D. 24. 2. 2.) A *liberta* who has married a *patronus* cannot divorce herself from him without his consent, unless she has been manumitted *ex causa fideicommissi.* (D. 24. 2. 10.)

death of his daughter Tullia. Wives also left their husbands on equally trivial pretexts, and permanent separation might be made by common consent.

*Sic fiunt octo mariti*
*Quinque per autumnos.*

Juven. *Sat.* 6. 229.

*Aut minus, aut certe non plus, tricesima lux est,*
*Et nubit decimo jam Thelesina viro.*

Martial, *Epi.* 6. 7.

See Heineccii *Antiq. Roman.* p. 130.

In 886 A.D. Leo the Philosopher first declared ecclesiastical benediction to be necessary to marriage (in the Eastern Empire).

*Legitimation.* Children born *extra matrimonium* (*spurii*, Gai. I. 64) may be made legitimate, 1, by the subsequent marriage of their parents, if they had the *connubium* at the time of conception, and the children ratify the legitimation. This form was introduced by Constantine the Great. The validity of the marriage must be attested by an *instrumentum dotale* (containing the agreement as to the *dos*). 2. *Per oblationem curiæ*, by becoming, or marrying, *a decurio** (introduced by Theodosius II. and Valentinian). 3. By imperial rescript (74th Novel). It was not granted if there were any legitimate children of the same parents, nor unless marriage had become impossible. 4. By will (Novels).

See under *Donatio* and *Dos*, p. 83, and Appendix, p. 207; also *Ancient Law*, p. 154.

* The senates of the independent towns (*municipia*) were called *curiæ*, and the senators *decuriones*. In the time of Trajan the office was undertaken with great reluctance, and its duties were sometimes inflicted as a punishment. In 442 Theodosius and Valentinian held out the gift of legitimation as an inducement to accept the labour and expense of the position. But the legitimation carried with it legal relationship to the father only, and not to the rest of the family. See C. 5. 27. 3 and 9; also the Novels, 89. 2—7.

## OF ADOPTION AND ARROGATION.

Inst. I. 11. Gai. I. 98—107; II. 136—138; III. 83, 84.

Adoption consists in transferring one father's children into the power of another. It is one of the fictions used by the Romans to create an artificial extension of the family. 1. By authority of a magistrate. 2. Before the people. 3. By imperial rescript.

Gaius says, *Adoptio duobus modis fit, aut populi auctoritate, aut imperio magistratus, velut Prætoris.* (I. 98.)

*Arrogatio** is the adoption of persons who are *sui juris. Populi auctoritate adoptamus eos qui sui juris sunt: quæ species adoptionis dicitur adrogatio, quia et is qui adoptat rogatur, id est interrogatur an velit eum quem adoptaturus sit justum sibi filium esse; et is qui adoptatur rogatur an id fieri patiatur; et populus rogatur an id fieri jubeat.*† Three con-

* *Arrogationes* (says Aulus Gellius) *non temerè nec inexploratè committuntur: nam comitia, arbitris etiam pontificibus, præbentur, quæ curiata appellantur.*

† *Imperio magistratus adoptamus eos qui in potestate parentium sunt. . . . Illa adoptio quæ per populum fit nusquam nisi Romæ fit: at hac etiam in provinciis apud Præsides earum fieri solet. Per populum feminæ non adoptantur* (as Aulus Gellius

ditions: 1, the arrogator must give security to a public officer that if the arrogated son dies before puberty, he will restore his property to his heirs; 2, if he is emancipated without just cause or disinherited before puberty, the *arrogator* must not only restore the son's property but add a fourth of his own (*quarta D. Pii*, or *quarta Antonina*); 3, the son on attaining puberty can rescind the arrogation, if prejudicial.

*Adoptio* is, 1, *plena*, when the adoptor is an ascendant of the child adopted and acquires *patria potestas* over him; 2, *minus plena*, when being adopted by a collateral or an *extraneus* (*i.e.*, one outside the family) he remains in the family of his natural father, but has a right of succession to his adoptive father, if he dies intestate. Thus (under Justinian) the natural father loses none of his rights or liabilities in respect of the child given in adoption *minus plena*. But by the old law, the adoptor always acquired *patria potestas* over the adopted child.

says: *quoniam cum feminis nulla comitiorum communio est*): *apud Prætorem vero vel in provinciis apud Proconsulem Legatumve etiam feminæ solent adoptari. Item impuberem apud populum adoptari aliquando prohibitum est, aliquando* (if there were *justa causa*, and on certain conditions) *permissum est. Apud Prætorem vero, cujuscunque ætatis adoptare possumus.* (Gai. I. 99—102).

From the time of Diocletian, arrogation was effected by imperial rescript, instead of *per populum*.

*Adoptio naturam imitatur.* An adopted son much resembles a son born in marriage.* The adoptor must be eighteen years older than the adopted. (This was a doubtful point in the time of Gaius.) He cannot adopt *ad diem*. He must be a Roman citizen. Women can only adopt by the indulgence of the emperor (since the time of Diocletian) when they have lost their own children. Gaius says, *feminæ nullo modo adoptare possunt, quia ne quidem naturales liberos in potestate habent.* (I. 104.) But *spadones* may adopt. A person may adopt another as a grandson though he has no son; if he has a son, he must have the son's consent. A person arrogated having children, submits them to the power of the arrogator. A freedman can be adopted by no one but his patron, and only when *he* has no descendants. Slaves become free by adoption, but do not thereby acquire the rights of a son.

A person adopted, or entering the family of his adoptor, takes the adoptor's name, at the same time adding his own in the form of an adjective, *e.g.*, Octavius adopted by Cæsar is called *Cæsar Octavianus*.

See *Ancient Law*, p. 130.

* "The fiction of adoption so closely simulates the reality of kinship, that neither law nor opinion makes the slightest difference between a real and an adoptive connexion." (*Ancient Law*, p. 133.)

## OF EMANCIPATIO.

Inst. I. 12. Gai. I. 116—122, 132—141.

By the old law emancipation from the *patria potestas* was effected by three fictitious sales *per æs et libram*—with the copper and scales—followed by manumission. For an account of sale by *mancipatio*, see Gai. I. 119—122, and *Ancient Law*, p. 204. Three sales were required only in the case of a son. All other descendants might be emancipated by one sale. After the final sale the friendly purchaser might either manumit the child himself, or re-sell him to his father for that purpose. In the former case he was called *manumissor extraneus*, and had the right of a patron, but a contract was made between him and the father (*contracta fiducia*), binding him to re-sell or to reserve the father's rights, failing which contract the prætor would give the *bonorum possessio unde decem personæ* (p. 136). In 503 A.D., Anastasius allowed emancipation to be effected by imperial rescript, requiring only the consent of the children, and not their presence as before. Justinian substitutes a solemn declaration before a magistrate.

A son or daughter emancipated from the power of their father, or a wife from the *manus* of her husband (but not yet manumitted), were said to be *in mancipio:* and as *manus* resembled *patria potestas* (Gai. I. 109), so *mancipium* was very analogous to slavery. But a person *in mancipio* could never become the subject of property, like a slave, nor did the laws restricting the enfranchisement of slavery apply in his case. He is, however, said to be *loco servi,* though a woman who makes a *coemptio* (another form of fictitious sale) is not reduced *in servilem conditionem. Ii qui in causa mancipii sunt, quia servorum loco habentur, vindicta, censu, testamento manumissi sui juris fiunt* (Gai. I. 138). *Ac ne diu quidem in eo jure detinentur homines, sed plerumque hoc fit dicis causa uno momento; nisi scilicet ex noxali causâ* (p. 188) *manciparentur.* (I. 141.)

A parent has the same rights over the goods of those whom he emancipates, as a *patronus* over those of his *libertus* (see p. 132). So if they are under puberty, he becomes their tutor. The benefit of emancipation may be lost by the child's ingratitude. A parent may emancipate a son and retain a grandson by that son, and *vice versâ.* Children, whether natural or adoptive, have hardly any means of enforcing emancipation, unless cruelly treated by their parent. A child cannot be emancipated against his will.

## OF CAPITIS DEMINUTIO.

Inst. I. 16. Gai. I. 158—163; III. 27, 51, 153.

*Capitis deminutio*, or *prioris status permutatio* (Gaius), is, 1, *maxima;* 2, *minor;* and 3, *minima.*

1. *Maxima* involves loss of *status* (i) *libertatis*, (ii) *civitatis*, (iii) *familiæ*, as *servitudo.*

2. *Minor*, of (ii) and (iii), as *deportatio.*

3. *Minima*, of (iii), only, as *emancipatio*, *adoptio.*

A person *capite minutus* is discharged from all *civil* debts previously incurred, but not from those arising from delicts. *Nemo delictis exuitur, quamvis capite minutus sit.* (D. 4. 5. 2. 3.) The prætor, however, gives relief to the creditor, and the debtor is always *naturaliter obligatus* (p. 161).

Change of dignity does not alter *status.**

* *Status* may be taken to mean the powers, duties, and privileges—the personal conditions—anciently residing in the Roman family. (*Ancient Law*, p. 170.) *Status* and *caput* are not synonymous terms, for a condition or *status* is repeatedly ascribed to a slave, and yet it is affirmed that he has "*nullum caput.*" Austin, therefore, thinks that *caput* signifies certain conditions which are *capital* or principal (such as Liberty and Citizenship), and which cannot be acquired or lost without a conspicuous change in the legal position of the party. (See Austin, Lectures 12 and 42.) Niebuhr and Savigny think that the word *caput* was originally used for the entry of a citizen's name on the register of the census. This would be expunged on a loss of *civitas* or *libertas*, and altered on a change of *familia.*

*Agnatio* (p. 58) is generally * (Gaius makes no exception) destroyed by every *capitis deminutio*. *Cognatio* is lost only by *maxima* and *minor* (Justinian); Gaius says it is never destroyed, *quia civilis ratio civilia quidem jura corrumpere potest, naturalia vero non potest.* (Gai. I. 158.) *Servile caput nullum jus habet, ideo nec minui potest.* (Paul, D. 4. 5. 3.)

By the old law every *capitis deminutio* destroyed the rights of use and usufruct (Paul, *Sent.* III. 6), the general result being that *prior persona evanescit.* By Justinian's law only *maxima* and *minor* extinguish personal servitudes. (Inst. II. 4. 3 and C. 3. 33. 16.)

A will also is made invalid by the *capitis deminutio* of the testator.

## OF TUTORS AND CURATORS.

Inst. I. 13—15, 17—26. Gai. I. 143—157, 164—200.

*Tutela* is an authority given by the civil law over a person *sui juris* under puberty, to protect

* By a constitution of Anastasius of 498 A.D. it is declared: *Fratrem emancipatum etiam ad legitimam fratrum et sororum, necnon liberorum fratrum tutelam, quasi minime patris potestate per jus emancipationis relaxatus, si non alia juri cognita excusatione munitus sit vocari; nec sub prætextu capitis deminutionis alienum ab hujusmodi onere semetipsum esse contendere sancimus.* (C. 5. 30. 4. See also Inst. III. 5.)

his tender age. *Sed impuberes quidem in tutela esse omnium civitatium jure contingit; quia id naturali rationi conveniens est, ut is qui perfectæ ætatis non sit alterius tutela regatur. Nec fere ulla civitas est, in qua non licet parentibus liberos suis impuberibus testamento tutorem dare: quamvis, ut supra diximus, soli cives Romani videantur tantùm liberos in potestate habere.* Gai. I. 189. It is, 1, *testamentaria;* 2, *legitima;* 3, *fiduciaria;* 4, *dativa;* and 5, *muliebris.*

1. *Fundamentum testamentariæ tutelæ erat patria potestas. Tutela* supplies the place of *patria potestas. Tutor auctor fit.** A parent may appoint a tutor by will for descendants in his power, provided that at his death they become *sui juris,* and are under puberty. Also for posthumous children.

*Who may be testamentary tutors?* Anyone with whom the testator has *testamenti factio* (*vide* p. 93), and who can discharge public offices; but not uncertain persons, nor women (without special grant), nor slaves, unless enfranchised at the same, nor *furiosi.* The tutor must have completed twenty-five years and be of sound mind, and he may be appointed to or from a particular

* The imperfection of the individual in the early part of his existence was supplied in the Roman system by *patria potestas,* and failing that, by *tutela.*

time, or on a condition, but not for a special purpose. A person under *patria potestas* may be appointed tutor. *Dari potest tutor, non sȯlum paterfamilias, sed etiam filiusfamilias.*

2. *Legitima tutela.* In default of appointment by will, the nearest *agnatus* or nearest degree of agnates* become tutors-at-law. *Plerumque ubi*

* The *agnati* are relations by unbroken descent through males. *Sunt autem agnati per virilis sexus personas cognatione juncti, quasi a patre agnati* (Gai. I. 156). They are the members of the same civil family as held together by the *patria potestas* of the *paterfamilias*, or who would have been under his power if born in his life-time. Adoption, as well as marriage, creates agnates, because it places the adopted under the *patria potestas* of the head of the family. "*Cognatic* relationship is simply the conception of kinship familiar to modern ideas; it is the relationship arising through common descent from the same pair of married persons, whether the descent be traced through males or females. *Agnatic* relationship is something very different: it excludes a number of persons whom we in our day should certainly consider of kin to ourselves, and it includes many more whom we should never reckon among our kindred." "In the first place, they (the Agnates) are all the Cognates who trace their connection exclusively through males. A table of Cognates is, of course, formed by taking each lineal ancestor in turn, and including all his descendants of both sexes in the tabular view; if then, in tracing the various branches of such a genealogical table or tree, we stop whenever we come to the name of a female, and pursue that particular branch or ramification no further, all who remain after the descendants of women have been excluded are Agnates, and their connection together is Agnatic Relationship." "The foundation of Agnation is not the marriage of Father and Mother, but the authority of the Father." "The Prætors early laid hold on Cognation as the

*successionis est emolumentum, ibi et tutelæ onus esse debet.** (Inst. I. 17.) By the Novels of Justinian (118) the *tutela legitima* devolves on the nearest male blood relation, the distinction between *agnati* and *cognati* being abolished (*vide* p. 138.) By the law of the Twelve Tables, women also had agnates for tutors, but this *tutela* was abolished by the *Lex Claudia.* While it lasted, agnates who were *legitimi tutores* might transfer such tutelage to others by *in jure cessio* (*tutor cessicius*).

If a parent emancipates a descendant under puberty, he becomes his tutor-at-law.

The *legitima tutela* of freedmen belongs to the patron, or his children (if over twenty-five years of age).

3. *Tutela fiduciaria.* Under the old law (see p. 53) the person emancipated was enfranchised either by the father himself or by the fictitious purchaser, who was then called *manumissor extraneus.* In the latter case the *manumissor extraneus* acquired the rights of a patron, and

*natural* form of kinship, and spared no pains in purifying their system from the older conception." See *Ancient Law*, pp. 146—152. *Cognationem facit etiam adoptio: etenim quibus fiet agnatus hic qui adoptatus est, iisdem etiam cognatus fiet.* (Ulpian, D. 38. 8. 1. 4.)

* In English law the guardianship devolves on the next of kin who will *not* succeed.

became *tutor fiduciarius* to the emancipated child (if under puberty). So a *coemptionator*, in the case of *coemptio* (Gai. I. 166, 167, 172, 175, 195). Under Justinian *tutela fiduciaria* occurs in the case of descendants under puberty who have been emancipated by an ascendant who is dead. *E.g.*, a father becomes fiduciary tutor to a son emancipated by the grandfather, a brother to an emancipated brother, or a paternal uncle to an emancipated nephew.

4. *Tutela dativa.* Tutors are appointed by magistrates, 1, when there is no *tutor testamentarius* or *legitimus*; 2, when a testamentary tutor has been appointed for a particular time or purpose which has elapsed or is accomplished; 3, when he is excused, removed, or taken captive.

*How appointed?* Under the *Lex Atilia*, at Rome, by the *prætor urbanus* and a majority of the tribunes; afterwards, also, by the city præfect, or the *defensores* (if the pupil's property did not exceed 500 *solidi*): * under the *Lex Julia et Titia*, in the provinces, by the *præsides.*

Gaius says that women may apply for a tutor in the place of one who is absent, and on his appointment, *prior desinit.* Not so a freedwoman. (I. 173, 174.)

* The *solidus*, formerly called *aureus*, was nearly equivalent to the English guinea.

5. *Tutela muliebris* (Gaius). By the old law women *sui juris* were obliged to have tutors not only till the age of puberty but for life, as the ancients thought, because of the weakness of their intellect, *propter animi levitatem;* for "a sex created to please and obey was never supposed to have attained the age of reason and experience" (Gibbon). Gaius says: "But there seems to be no appreciable reason to account for the tutelage of women of full age. The one commonly assigned —that being so often imposed upon through their weakness of mind, it was only right that they should be subjected to the authority of tutors—is more specious than true. For women of full age manage their own affairs for themselves, and in some transactions the tutor supplies his authority merely as a matter of form; in many cases the magistrate even compels him to do so against his will. For this reason a woman cannot bring an action against her tutor on account of his tutelage. But in the case of *pupils* of either sex, the tutors who administer their affairs may have to give an account in a court of law, when their wards have grown up to puberty." "There is no instance of such female tutelage existing among foreign nations, but there is often something analogous to it, as, for instance, in Bithynia, where, if a woman makes a contract, her hus-

band or grown-up son must, by law, give his authority." (I. 190—193.) Ulpian accounts for it *propter sexus infirmitatem et propter forensium rerum ignorantiam.* (*Reg. Juris*, XI. 1.) Cicero supports the institution, and complains that *quum multa præclare legibus essent constituta, ea jurecon-sultorum ingeniis corrupta ac depravata sunt. Mulieres omnes propter infirmitatem consilii majores in tutorum potestate esse voluerunt: hi invenerunt genera tutorum, quæ potestate mulierum continerentur* (*Pro Muræna*, c. 12). A wife *in manu* might have a limited or unlimited (*plena* or *angusta*) choice of a tutor given her by her husband's will —*tutor optivus.* By the *Lex Papia Poppæa* free-born women were released from tutelage by the right of three children; freedwomen by that of four, if they were in the *legitima tutela* of their patron or his children. But this *tutela muliebris* gradually disappeared, and is not noticed by Justinian.*

* The Perpetual Guardianship of women is "obviously neither more nor less than an artificial prolongation of the Patria Potestas." "The discovery of the manuscript of Gaius discloses this tutelage to us at a most interesting epoch, just when it had fallen into complete discredit, and was verging on extinction. The great jurisconsult himself scouts the popular apology offered for it in the mental inferiority of the female sex, and a considerable part of his volume is taken up with descriptions of the numerous expedients, some of them displaying extraordinary ingenuity, which the Roman lawyers had devised

*The duties of a tutor* are, (1) *negotia gerere*, to administer the property of his ward, and (2) *auctoritatem interponere.* But *mulierum tutores auctoritatem dumtaxat interponunt* (Ulpian).

*The auctoritas of tutors.* Up to seven a pupil (*infans*) has no *intellectus*, and the tutor acts alone. From seven to puberty, the pupil, having *intellectus* but not *judicium*, may make his condition better, but not worse, without the authority and presence of the tutor. The tutor's *auctoritas*, therefore, supplies (*auget*) the pupil's want of capacity to complete the solemnities of a legal transaction. Without this, a pupil cannot enter on or repudiate an inheritance, apply for *bonorum possessio*, or take an inheritance *ex fideicommisso*, nor can the authority be given after the conclusion of a transaction, nor by letter, nor in a matter in which the tutor is personally interested. *In his causis ex quibus obligationes mutuæ nascuntur, ut*

for enabling women to defeat the ancient rules. Led by the theory of Natural Law, the jurisconsults had evidently assumed the equality of the sexes as a principle of their code of equity. The restrictions which they attached were, it is to be observed, restrictions on the disposition of property, for which the assent of the woman's guardians was still formally required. Control of her person was apparently quite obsolete.

"Ancient law subordinates the woman to her blood relations, while a prime phenomenon of modern jurisprudence has been her subordination to her husband." (For the history of the change, see *Ancient Law*, p. 154).

*in emptionibus, venditionibus, locationibus, conductionibus, mandatis, depositis, si tutoris auctoritas non interveniat, ipsi quidem qui cum his contrahunt, obligantur; at invicem pupilli non obligantur.* (Inst. I. 21, pr.)

Tutors may be compelled to account for their pupils' property by the *actio tutelæ directa*, and they have in turn the *actio tutelæ contraria* against their pupils. If a suit is instituted between tutor and pupil, a curator is appointed *ad litem.*

*Termination of tutela.* *Tutela* is ended, 1, on the part of the pupil (i) by arriving at puberty, (ii) by death, (iii) by *capitis deminutio maxima, minor* and *minima*: 2, on the part of the tutor (i) by death, (ii) by *capitis deminutio maxima* or *minor*, but only *minima* in the case of *legitima tutela*, (iii) by excuse or removal, (iv) by expiration of term or fulfilment of object.

*Curators.* Pupils who are *sui juris* may, on arriving at puberty, receive curators, whose office begins at the age when the tutor's ceases. These curators are appointed by the same magistrates as tutors, but their duties are confined to the *property* of their wards. *Tutor datur personæ, curator rei vel causæ.* A curator cannot be appointed by will, but may be named by a testator, and confirmed by a magistrate. A curator holds office till the adolescent has completed his twenty-fifth year (*perfecta ætas*), unless he obtains a *venia ætatis*, or dispensation from the emperor. No one need have a curator against his will, except prodigals, madmen, persons of unsound mind, deaf, dumb, or incurably diseased (even after twenty-five), and pupils whose tutors are unfit or ill.

*Tutores* and *curatores legitimi*, or appointed by inferior magistrates (*sine inquisitione*), must find sureties to guarantee their good faith. Not so testamentary tutors.

*Excuses for exemption of tutors and curators.* 1. *Propter officium*, as military service, public office, or a liberal profession. 2. *Propter existimationis periculum*, as by alleging a law-suit with pupil, by having deadly enmity against his father, by husband being appointed curator to wife, or by being debtor or creditor of pupil. 3. *Propter impotentiam*, as by having three such offices in different families, by great poverty, by illness, by inability to read, by being above seventy or under twenty-five. Also by having three children (not adopted) in Rome, four in Italy, and five in the provinces, who are alive, or have fallen in battle, for then "glory renders them immortal." Grand-children by a son are reckoned as children. A tutor is not obliged to become the curator of the same person against his will.

If one of several acts alone, he is called "*onerarius;*" but he must give security to the rest (*honorarii*), who are still responsible.

*How removed.* At Rome, by the prætor; in the provinces, by the *præsides*, or legates of the proconsul. An accusation is open to all but *impuberes*, the office being suspended during the proceedings. A tutor who does not maintain his pupil may be removed. A suspected person removed for fraud is rendered infamous, but not for neglect. A tutor or curator is only bound to apply the same care in the duties of his office which he would use in the management of his own affairs.

See *Ancient Law*, pp. 160—162.

The Privilege of Three Children.

See pp. 62, 65, 128.

# BOOK II.—OF THINGS.

Inst. II. 1. 2. Gai. II. 1—25, 66—79.

*Res*, in the language of Roman lawyers are (1), Things, Persons, Acts (or Forbearances), as subjects or objects of rights and obligations; and (2), Rights and Obligations themselves. (Austin.) They are, I. *In nostro patrimonio*, belonging to individuals; II. *Extra nostrum patrimonium:* 1, *communes;* 2, *publicæ;* 3, *universitatis;* and 4, *nullius*. Gaius adds a *summa divisio* of things (a) *divini juris* and (b) *humani*.

1. *Res communes* are things which are common to all the world, as air, running water, the sea and its shores.

2. *Res publicæ* are things which belong to all the inhabitants of a particular country.

3. *Res universitatis* are the property of corporations, as theatres and race-courses.

4. *Res nullius* are things consecrated (*sacræ*), inviolable (*sanctæ*), as the walls and gates of a city, or *religiosæ*, as burial grounds; also things unappropriated, as unoccupied land, or wild animals.

*Res* are also III. *Corporales*, or tangible (1, Movable; and 2, Immovable); and IV. *Incor-*

*porales*, or intangible (a division of the Stoics); V. *Mancipi*, requiring solemn forms of conveyance, as estates and houses in Italy, rural servitudes, slaves, and domestic animals; and VI. *Nec mancipi*, being capable of alienation by simple transfer. The last distinction is abolished by Justinian.

Ownership (*dominium*)* consists in, 1, the *jus utendi* (using all the services the thing possessed can render); 2, *jus fruendi* (taking its fruits and products); 3, *abutendi* (alienating or destroying it); 4, *vindicandi* (recovering it from the hands of another). It is I. *Quiritarium*, and II. *bonitarium*.†

*Possession* is (1), natural; and (2), civil. 1. Natural possession is the physical detention of an object without the right or *animus* of an owner. 2.

* "In the Institutes of Gaius and Justinian, the right of property or dominion is not defined at all. Things are described; the modes of acquiring property in them are described; servitudes are described; but of the right of property or dominion no direct description is given. The nature of the right (in respect of the power of user) is left to be inferred from the treatise generally."

"The right of property (or *dominium*), pre-eminently so called, is a right of unlimited duration; that is to say, there is no person having any interest in the subject subsequent to his own, from whom the owner may not divert it by a total or partial alienation. Let the contingent successors be who they may, they have no such right in the subject as the owner may not defeat, and as sets a restriction on his power of using the subject." Austin, Lect. 48.

† Gai. II. 40. This distinction is abolished in the Novels.

Civil possession is the detention, sometimes not physical, of a thing acquired *ex justa causa* (*i.e.*, *nec vi*, *nec clam*, *nec precario*), and with the intention to hold the thing detained as one's own. *Aliud est possidere, longè aliud in possessione esse.* (Ulpian.) Possession may be ripened into *dominium* by *usucapio* (p. 80), on the conditions of *justa causa* and *bona fides*. *Differentia inter dominium et possessionem hæc est quod dominium nihilo minus ejus manet qui dominus esse non vult, possessio autem recedit ut quisque constituit nolle possidere.* (D. 41. 2. 27.)

*Dominium* is acquired by individuals, I. *Jure gentium:* by 1, *occupatio;* 2, *accessio*; and 3, *traditio:* and II. *Jure civili:* by 1, *mancipatio;* 2, *in jure cessio;* 3, *traditio;* 4, *usucapio* and *præscriptio*; 5, *adjudicatio;* and 6, *lex.*

I. *Jure gentium*, by the Law of Nations. 1. *Occupatio* is the appropriation of a thing which has no owner. *Res nullius cedit occupanti.* Such are wild beasts, birds and fish, even when caught on another man's land. But if only wounded, no property is acquired in them. Bees must be hived before they can be acquired. Peacocks, pigeons, and deer are naturally wild, but belong to their owner as long as they stray *animo revertendi* (*i.e.*, retain the habit of returning). Fowls and geese are tame creatures, and remain the property of their owner, though they stray from home. Captives and spoil taken in war belong to the captor till they escape. Pearls, gems, and precious stones, found on the sea-shore, belong to the finder.

2. *Accessio* is a mode of acquiring property by the increase or development of a thing in one's possession. It is (i) natural, and (ii) industrial.

(i) Natural accession occurs (a) by the offspring of slaves or animals, (b) by the deposit of alluvial soil by a river, (c) by land acquired by the force of a river, (d) by an island rising in a river, (e) by the desertion of its channel by a river.

An island rising in the sea belongs to the first occupant; but rising in the middle of a river, it belongs equally to the riparian owners; and if nearer to one bank than another, to the nearest proprietor. An island made by a river cutting off a piece of land belongs to its former owner. If a river changes its channel, the old bed belongs to the riparian owners. An inundation effects no change of property.

(ii) Industrial accessions are (a) *specificatio*, the production of a new species from another's materials or on another's property; (b) *commixtio*, the junction of things separable or inseparable. If the new species can be restored to its old materials, the owner of the materials is the owner of the thing made; if not, the maker is the owner, but he must give satisfaction to the owner of the materials. So if a man makes a thing partly of his own materials, and partly of another's. If two things are mixed together with the consent of the owners, as wine or molten gold, whether they can be separated or not, the product is common property; but if without consent, and separable, the property is distinct. A building accedes to the soil on which it is built, *superficies solo cedit;* but if built by *bonâ fide* mistake on another's ground, the owner of the materials may claim them or their value, together with the cost of the work. A plant which has taken root accedes to the soil in which it is planted. So writing accedes to the paper on which it is written; but a painting on another man's canvas belongs to the painter. The young of animals, if appropriated, belong to the usufructuary; but the children of slaves become the property of the owner of the mother. Fruits belong to the land until the usufructuary has gathered them. Treasure found on a man's own ground, or by chance in a consecrated or religious place, belong to the finder. If found by chance on another man's ground, half belongs to the finder and half to the owner of the soil.

3. *Traditio*, or transfer. Four requisites for complete transfer of property: (i) the transferor

must be the owner, or one duly authorised by him; (ii) he must place the transferee in legal possession of the thing; (iii) he must have the *intentio* to pass the property in it; (iv) the transferee must have the *intentio* to become the owner. *Nihil tam conveniens est naturali æquitati quam voluntatem domini, volentis rem suam in alium transferre, ratam haberi.* (Gaius, D. 41. 1. 9. 3.) Property is not acquired by the buyer till the price is paid or secured. *Nunquam nuda traditio transfert dominium; sed ita, si venditio, aut aliqua justa causa præcesserit, propter quam traditio sequeretur.* (Paul, D. 41. 1. 31 pr.) The thing transferred must be susceptible of private ownership.

Things abandoned (except in a storm) pass to the first occupant by *quasi traditio.*

II. *Jure civili*, by the Quiritarian law of Rome. 1. *Mancipatio* is the transfer of a *res corporalis* by a fictitious sale with solemn forms, in the presence of a *libripens* and five Roman citizens.* 2. *In*

* See Gaius I. 119—122. The word *nexum* was used to signify any conveyance of property *per æs et libram*, with copper and scales. It afterwards came insensibly to denote also a contract. (*Ancient Law*, p. 315.) Festus says: *Nexum est, ut ait Gallus Ælius, quodcumque per æs et libram geritur, idque necti dicitur. Nexum æs apud antiquos dicebatur pecunia quæ per nexum obligatur.* Heineccius says: *Jungitur sæpe mancipio nexus vel traditio nexu. Mancipium transfert dominium juris Quiritium: Nexu res tantum obligatur,* e.g., *ut aliquis in ea jus pignoris vel simile haberet.*

*jure cessio* is a fictitious suit, in which the seller of a *res corporalis* allows it to be adjudged (*addici*) to the buyer by collusion. Ulpian thus describes it, *In jure cessio fit per tres personas, in jure cedentis, vindicantis, addicentis. In jure cedit dominus; vindicat is cui ceditur; addicit Prætor. Reg.* 19. 9. 3. *Traditio*, or transfer, includes the forms of *donatio*, or gift, *sub coronâ emptio*, or sale of captives, public auction (*sub hastâ*), &c. 4. *Usucapio*, *vide* p. 80. 5. *Adjudicatio* is the decision of a judge in a suit to divide an inheritance (*familiæ erciscendæ*), or common property (*communi dividundo*), or to fix the limits of property (*finium regundorum*). 6. *Lex.* Property may be acquired by a special direction of the civil law, as in the case of a legacy.

*Vide* Appendix, p. 209, and *Ancient Law*, chap. 8.

## OF SERVITUDES.

Inst. II. 3—5. Gai. II. 29—33, 86.

A servitude is the liability of the property of one person to certain rights of another estate or person over it. A *right* of servitude is a right to enjoy in a given or definite manner a subject owned by another.

*Servitus* is used to mean (1) the liability, and (2) the right, to a servitude.

Servitudes are, I. Prædial, or real (*prædiorum, sive rerum*); and, II. Personal (*personarum, sive hominum*).

I. Prædial servitudes are the liabilities of one estate or building (*res serviens*) to the superior rights of another estate or building (*res dominans*), such superior rights residing in the owner or occupier of the *prædium* for the time being. *Prædium servit prædio.** No one can acquire a prædial servitude unless he possesses a *prædium*. *Nulli res sua servit*. A man cannot enjoy a servitude on his own property, for this would involve *consolidatio*, or merger. *Servitus servitutis esse non potest*. There cannot be a servitude of a servitude. Thus a legacy of an usufruct in a right of way would be ineffectual. For the right of servitude being a fraction or modification of the right of property can only exist over a *res corporalis*. Servitudes, considered as liabilities, are of a passive, not an active nature. *Servitutum non ea natura est ut aliquid faciat quis, . . . sed ut aliquid patiatur vel non faciat*. (D. 8. 1. 15.) But *rights* of servitude may consist *in faciendo, in habendo, in prohibendo*. A *positive* servitude consists *in patiendo*, a *negative*

* The right is spoken of as if it resided in the inanimate *prædium* itself instead of its owner. "The *prædium* is erected into a legal or fictitious *person*, and is styled *prædium dominans*." So the *prædium serviens*. (Austin, Lect. 50.)

*in non faciendo.* A positive servitude restricts the owner's right of exclusion and user, a negative servitude merely restricts his right of user. (Austin.) A servitude must be enjoyed *civiliter, i.e.*, within reasonable limits. The owner of the *res serviens* is not bound to keep it in repair. The right to a servitude is indivisible. A real may be turned into a personal servitude.

Prædial servitudes are, 1, rural, affecting the land itself, as the right of pathway (*iter*), driving cattle or vehicles (*actus*), road (*via*), or aqueduct (*aquæductus*); 2, urban, or attached to buildings raised on the soil, as (on the part of the *res dominans*) the right of support from a contiguous house (*jus oneris ferendi*), of fixing a beam in a neighbour's wall (*jus tigni immittendi*), or (on the part of the *res serviens*) the liability to receive rain-water from roof or gutter (*jus stillicidii vel fluminis recipiendi*), and prevention from raising a house too high and obstructing light and view (*jus altius non tollendi et non officiendi luminibus vel prospectui*). Rural servitudes are *res mancipi*: urban are *res nec mancipi*.

II. Personal servitudes, or rights of servitude, are those which are enjoyed immediately by a particular person, without being attached to an estate. They reside in a given person, *not* as being the owner or occupier of a given parcel of land. They are servitudes *in gross*, or are annexed to the persons of the parties in whom they reside; while real servitudes are "appurtenant" to lands. (Austin.)

*How servitudes acquired.** Under the old law, in the case of estates in Italy, by, 1, *mancipatio* (for *res mancipi* only); 2, *in jure cessio* (the only form for urban servitudes). In the case of provincial lands, by agreements and stipulations only. But when (1) and (2) disappeared, by 1, *quasi-traditio* (by the *jus prætorium*, as there could be no *traditio* of a *res incorporalis*); 2, will; 3, *usucapio* and *præscriptio*; 4, agreement; 5, reservation of the servitude in a transfer of the prædium (*deductio*); 6, *adjudicatio*; and 7, *lex*.

*How ended.* 1, by destruction of *res serviens* or *res dominans*; 2, by merger, or consolidation of servitude and *proprietas* in one person; 3, by release by the owner of *res dominans*; 4, by non-user (ten years if owner present, twenty if absent).†

*Usufructus* is the right of *using* and *enjoying* the fruits of things belonging to others without destroying their substance (*salvâ rerum substantiâ*).

* Gaius touches upon servitudes only in relation to the mode of their transfer.

† By the old law *viam, iter, actum, aquæductum, qui biennio usus non est, amisisse videtur.* (Paul, *Sent.* I. 17.)

Thus the usufructuary takes the wool, milk, and offspring of animals, the skill of a slave, or the produce of mines and quarries. He cannot cut down forest trees, except for necessary works, nor is he entitled to treasure found on the land, to the children of slaves, nor to alluvial land. He must keep buildings in repair, and maintain the numbers of the slaves and live stock. (D. 7. 1. 9. &c.)

Property divested of *usufructus* is called *nuda proprietas;* but the proprietor (*dominus*) retains the *jus abutendi* and *vindicandi.* He may also require security from the usufructuary. The usufructuary must take possession of the fruits, as otherwise they remain to the *dominus.*

*How acquired.* In the time of Gaius, by *in jure cessio;* in the time of Justinian, by, 1, contract (*traditio, deductio,* or *pactiones et stipulationes*); 2, will; 3, *adjudicatio;* 4, *lex.*

*How ended.* By, 1, the death or *capitis deminutio* (*maxima* and *minor*) of the usufructuary; 2, expiration of the term; 3, non-user according to the manner and during the time fixed; 4, merger of usufruct and property; 5, destruction or transformation of the property; 6, renunciation of the right.

Usufruct applies properly only to things *quæ usu non consumuntur;* but there may be a *quasi* usufruct in *res fungibiles*, or things which can be replaced in like quality and quantity.

Usufruct, unlike personal servitudes, is susceptible of conditions and limitations, but it is indivisible.

A usufructuary cannot transfer more than his personal rights. But if a *filiusfamilias*, or slave, dies in the enjoyment of a usufruct, his father or master is entitled to it for life.

*Usus* is the right to use the property of another (*jus utendi*) without destroying its substance (*jus abutendi*) or enjoying its produce (*jus fruendi*), except for necessary supplies: hence it is called *nudus usus*. Acquired and ended in the same way as usufruct; but not transferable, nor divisible.

*Habitatio* is the right to live gratuitously in the house of another. Transferable, and not extinguished by non-user, nor by *capitis deminutio*. (In these respects it differed from *usus*.) Justinian declares *habitatio* to be a servitude. This had been a disputed point among the older writers.

*Emphyteusis** is the right to possess and enjoy

* The name of *emphyteusis* (given by the Emperor Zeno) appears to have arisen from the condition originally imposed on the emphyteuta of *planting* the land, ἐμφυτεύειν. It was a right closely analogous to an estate of inheritance in copyhold,

the lands or buildings of another for an unlimited period, subject to the payment of an annual rent (*pensio*). It is alienable, but a fine of over a 50th of the value is payable on alienation (see p. 156).

*Jus Pignoris et hypothecæ* is the right of a creditor over the property of his debtor, to secure a debt. *Pignus* applies to movables actually transferred to the pledgee; *hypotheca* only to immovables, the possession of which remains with the pledgor, or mortgagor, the creditor having a charge upon them.

*Superficies* is the right granted by an owner of land to another to build on it, without acquiring the soil. It is transferable. Austin calls this a species of *condominium*, or ownership in common, rather than a *jus in re alienâ*. He also says that *usufructus*, *usus*, *habitatio*, *superficies*, *emphyteusis*, and perhaps other rights which, in the language of the Roman law, are frequently styled servitudes, would be deemed (justly) by English lawyers rights of property for the life of the owner, or rights of property more nearly approaching in principle to an estate in fee simple, or absolute property in a personal chattel. Lect. 50.

and is supposed by some to have been the origin of feudalism. The prætor treated the emphyteuta as a true proprietor, whose rights, as a general rule, descended to his heirs, though limited by the original contract. See *Ancient Law*, p. 299; and Austin, Lect. 52.

## OF USUCAPIO AND PRÆSCRIPTIO.

Inst. II. 6. Gai. II. 40—61, 89; III. 80; IV. 36.

*Usucapio*, by the law of the XII Tables, was the acquisition of property by a *bonâ fide* use and uninterrupted possession extending to one year for movables, and two * for immovables (only in Italy), *ne rerum dominia diutius in incerto essent.*

*Præscriptio*, or *longi temporis possessio*, was the acquisition of immovables in the provinces by possession during ten years when the parties were present (*i. e.*, domiciled in the same province), and twenty years when absent.

Justinian abolishes all distinction between the two, fixing the limit at ten or twenty years for immovables, and at three years for movables.

*Conditions.* 1, *bonâ fide* possession, with *animus domini*, and founded on *justa causa*; † 2, continuance of uninterrupted possession for time fixed;

* In the case of *usucapio pro herede* and *usureceptio* (Gai. II. 52), possession for one year was sufficient even for those things *quæ solo continentur.*

† *Bona fides* is the reasonable belief of the possessor that he has lawfully acquired the property. Possession *ex justa causa* —on a good title—is one founded on a legal act, which shows that the last owner had the intention of parting with his proprietary rights and transferring them to another. "In order to

3, the things possessed must not be *extra commercium* (as things sacred, public, seized with violence, or stolen *).

Long possession, which has begun to run in favour of a deceased person, is continued in favour of the heir, or *bonorum possessor.*

Purchasers from the *fiscus* of property belonging to another, may repel the owner by an *exceptio* after five years' possession.

Gaius (II. 52-58) explains *usucapio pro herede* which is said to occur *si rem hereditariam cujus possessionem heres nondum nactus est, aliquis possederit.* The usucapion was allowed to take effect after a possession for one year even in the case of things *quæ solo continentur.* Gaius calls it unreasonable (*improba*), and traces it to the

have the benefit of Usucapion, it was necessary that the adverse possession should have begun in good faith, that is, with belief on the part of the possessor that he was lawfully acquiring the property; and it was further required that the commodity should have been transferred to him by some mode of alienation which, however unequal to conferring a complete title in the particular case, was at least recognised by the law. In the case, therefore, of a mancipation, however slovenly the performance might have been, yet, if it had been carried so far as to involve a Tradition or Delivery, the vice of the title would be cured by Usucapion in two years at most." "I know of nothing in the practice of the Romans which testifies so strongly to their legal genius as the use which they made of Usucapion." *Ancient Law*, p. 287.

* The *Lex Atinia* (196 B.C.) prohibited the acquisition of *res furtivæ*, and the *Lex Plautia* (88 B.C.) of *res vi possessæ.*

anxiety of the old Romans that the family rites should be performed, and that creditors should be paid their debts as quickly as possible. It was called "*lucrativa*," *nam sciens quisque rem alienam lucrifacit.* After the time of Hadrian, it took effect only in the case of a *heres necessarius* (p. 103).

Gaius also mentions *usureceptio*, by which an owner could recover property which he had transferred to another *fiduciæ causa* by usucapion extending only to one year even in the case of immovables. *Usureceptio est usu recipere quod aliquando suum fuit.* (Heineccius.) If the property had been pledged to secure a debt, the money must have been paid before the usucapion could operate, unless the debtor had hired the property from the creditor, or obtained it *precario* (subject to recall at will). In the case of the *populus* selling property pledged to it, the owner could recover against the purchaser (*prædiator*) by a possession extending to *two* years for immovables. Hence the common saying, "*ex prædiaturâ possessionem usurecipi.*" *Usurpatio* is the interruption of *usucapio.*

## OF DONATIO AND DOS.

### Inst. II. 7. Gai. II. 225.

*Donatio* is a transfer of property by gift. It may be, 1, *mortis causâ*, or 2, *inter vivos.*

1. *Donatio mortis causâ* must be made in contemplation of death, and to take effect only when death occurs. It may be made conditional on the death of a third person. It ranks with legacies. It is revocable at the pleasure of the donor, and lapses on the predecease of the donee.

Paul says (*Sententiæ*, II. 23): *Mortis causa donatio est quæ impendente metu mortis fit, ut est valetudinis, peregrinationis, navigationis vel belli. Mortis causa donat qui ad bellum proficiscitur, et qui navigat; ea scilicet condicione, ut si reversus fuerit, sibi restituatur; si perierit, penes eum remaneat cui donavit.* (III. 7.)

*Donatio mortis causa cessante valetudine et secuta sanitate et pœnitentia etiam revocatur: morte enim tantummodo convalescit* (it becomes valid). *Ib.*

2. *Donatio inter vivos* takes effect during the life of the donor, by the simple consent of the donee. It is revocable during the life of the donee, as for ingratitude, or on the unexpected birth of a child to the donor. If it exceeds 500 *solidi*, it must be registered by a public deed

except in the case of gifts to or from the Emperor, of money given for rebuilding a house destroyed by fire, or for the release of captives.

A *donatio ante nuptias* is the settlement made by a husband on his wife, and is conditional on a marriage taking effect. It belongs to the wife for life, but is managed by the husband, though it cannot be alienated by him even with her consent. It is brought in to meet the wife's *dos*, or dowry.

A *donatio propter nuptias* may be made during marriage as an addition to this settlement on the wife, or to her dowry. Any gifts other than an increase of the dowry or settlement are strictly forbidden between husband and wife, *ut ne conjuges ob mutuum amorem se invicem spoliarent*, to prevent their robbing each other from mutual affection. *Inter virum et uxorem donatio non valet, nisi certis ex causis, id est mortis causa, divortii causa servi manumittendi gratia.* The prohibition is an example of Customary Law introduced by the jurists (p. 7); *moribus apud nos receptum est, &c.* (D. 24. 1. 1.) Paul adds the following reason:—*nec esset eis studium liberos potius educendi.* Moreover, *sæpe futurum esset ut discuterentur matrimonia si non donaret is qui posset, atque ea ratione eventurum ut venalicia essent matrimonia.* (D. 24. 1. 2.) But gifts by which the donee is not enriched nor the donor impoverished are allowed. Thus necessary gifts of comfort and sustenance, or for repairs of buildings, trifles, and remuneratory presents may be made in addition to those above mentioned. Paul says, *Inter virum uxorem nec per interpositam personam donatio fieri potest*, and *contemplatione donationis imaginaria venditio contrahi non potest.* But *quocunque tempore contemplatione mortis inter virum et uxorem donatio facta est, morte secuta convalescit. Sent. Rec.* II. 23.

The following account of *Dos* is taken from Ulpian's *Regulæ*, Title 6, and Paul's *Sententiæ Receptæ*, II. 21:—

1. Dos aut datur, aut dicitur, aut promittitur.

2. Dotem dicere potest mulier quæ nuptura est, et debitor mulieris, si jussu ejus dicat; item parens mulieris virilis sexus, per virilem sexum cognatione junctus, velut pater, avus paternus. Dare, promittere dotem omnes possunt.

3. Dos aut profectitia dicitur, id est quam pater mulieris dedit; aut adventicia, id est ea quæ a quovis alio data est.

4. Mortuâ in matrimonio muliere dos a patre profecta ad patrem revertitur, quintis in singulos liberos in infinitum relictis penes virum. Quod si pater non sit, apud maritum remanet.

5. Adventicia autem dos semper penes maritum remanet, præterquam si is qui dedit, ut sibi

redderetur stipulatus fuit; quæ dos specialiter recepticia dicitur.

6. Divortio facto, si quidem sui juris sit mulier, ipsa habet actionem, id est dotis repetitionem; quod si in potestate patris sit, pater adjunctâ filiæ personâ habet actionem rei uxoriæ; nec interest adventicia sit dos, an profectitia.

7. Post divortium defunctâ muliere, heredi ejus actio non aliter datur, quam si moram in dote mulieri reddendâ maritus fecerit.

8. Dos si pondere numero mensurâ contineatur, annuâ bimâ trimâ die (within one, two, or three years) redditur; nisi ut præsens reddatur, convenerit. Reliquæ dotes statim redduntur.

9. Retentiones ex dote fiunt aut propter liberos, aut propter mores, aut propter impensas, aut propter res donatas, aut propter res amotas (carried off by the wife).

10. Propter liberos retentio fit, si culpâ mulieris aut patris cujus in potestate est divortium factum sit: tunc enim singulorum liberorum nomine sextæ retinentur ex dote; non plures tamen quam tres (*i.e.*, three-sixths). Sextæ in retentione sunt, non in petitione.

11. Dos quæ semel functa est amplius fungi non potest, nisi aliud matrimonium sit.

12. Morum nomine, graviorum quidem sexta retinetur; leviorum autem octava. Graviores

mores sunt adulteria tantum; leviores omnes reliqui.

13. Mariti mores puniuntur in ea quidem dote quæ a die reddi debet ita, ut propter majores mores præsentem dotem reddat, propter minores sexum mensium die (within six months). In ea autem quæ præsens reddi solet, tantum ex fructibus jubetur reddere, quantum in illa dote quæ triennio redditur repensatio facit.

14. Impensarum species sunt tres: aut enim necessariæ dicuntur, aut utiles, aut voluptuosæ.

15. Necessariæ sunt impensæ, quibus non factis dos deterior futura est, velut si quis ruinosas ædes refecerit.

16. Utiles sunt, quibus non factis quidem deterior dos non fuerit, factis autem fructuosior effecta est, veluti si vineta et oliveta fecerit.

17. Voluptuosæ sunt, quibus neque omissis deterior dos fieret, neque factis fructuosior effecta est; quod evenit in viridiariis (shrubberies) et picturis similibusque rebus.

Paul, *Sententiæ Receptæ*, II. 21:—

1. Dos aut antecedit aut sequitur matrimonium, et ideo vel ante nuptias vel post nuptias dari potest: sed ante nuptias data earum expectat adventum.

2. Lege Julia de adulteriis cavetur, ne dotale prædium maritus invitâ uxore alienet.

*Ib.*, 22 :—

1. Fructus fundi dotalis constante matrimonio percepti lucro mariti cedunt, etiam pro rata anni ejus quo factum est divortium.

When the *dos* was *data*, it was deposited with the *auspices* the day before the marriage. Among many nations *dotem maritus uxori, non uxor marito offerebat*, e.g., *apud Germanos*. (Heineccius.)

When a wife passed *in manum viri*, all her property went to her husband. In a marriage without *conventio in manum*, the wife's portion belongs to the husband during coverture, and he can, with her consent, sell or pledge her movable, but not her immovable property. On the wife's death it passes to her heirs, unless otherwise specified. If the husband has disposed of the movables he must restore an equivalent.

## OF ALIENATION.

Inst. II. 8. Gai. II. 62—65; 80—85.

In general the power of alienating property belongs only to the owner. But (says Gaius) *aliquando accidit, ut qui dominus sit alienandæ rei potestatem non habeat, et qui dominus non sit alienare possit.* Creditors, tutors, curators, and others may, in some cases, alienate property pledged or entrusted to them.

A husband cannot alienate his wife's immovable property, even with her consent; nor can it be seized by his creditors, *ne sexus muliebris fragilitas in perniciem substantiæ earum converteretur* (Inst. II. 8); and no pupil can alienate anything, although he may acquire, without the authority of his tutor.

Prodigals and madmen cannot part with their property.

In the time of Gaius, a woman could alienate a *res nec mancipi*, but not a *res mancipi*, without the *auctoritas* of her tutor, although she could receive either. But she could not release a debtor by the form of *acceptilatio* (p. 162). The Lex Julia, restraining the husband's power over his wife's immovables, was probably limited to estates in Italy. See Gai. II. 63. Justinian extends it to the provinces.

## OF ACQUIRING THROUGH OTHERS.

Inst. II. 9. Gai. II. 86—96; III. 163—167.

*Through whom.* 1. *Filiifamilias.* All that a son acquires with his father's property (*peculium profectitium*) belongs to the father; but what he acquires in any other way (*peculium adventitium*) belongs to the son, though the father has the usufruct. A father has no right to use or enjoy his son's *peculium castrense* (acquired in military service), or *quasi-castrense* (acquired in civil or ecclesiastical functions, or by the emperor's bounty). 2. Slaves can acquire only for their masters. If a slave is in the power of one man *in bonis*, and of another *ex jure Quiritium*, all that he acquires belongs to the owner *in bonis*, because he has the *potestas* (p. 41). (In the Novels, Justinian abolishes the difference between *dominium bonitarium* and *Quiritarium*.) A person under *potestas* can only enter on an inheritance by the command of his *paterfamilias* for whom he acquires it. *Possession* is also acquired through those in *potestas*, and through them usucapion takes effect. *Possessionem adquirimus et animo et corpore: animo utique nostro, corpore vel nostro vel alieno.* (Paul's *Sent. Rec.* V. 11.) A slave owned by several masters acquires for all according to their shares, unless his contract is specially limited. A man having merely the usufruct of a slave acquires only what is gained from his own property or the slave's labour. This extends to possession and usucapion. 3. *Extraneæ personæ* (persons not in the *familia*) must be duly authorised to act in the name and as agents of the acquirer.

## OF WILLS. (*Testamenta.*)

### Inst. II. 10—18, 22. Gai. II. 100—150, 174—190.

*Testamentum est justa sententia voluntatis nostræ, de eo quod quis post mortem suam fieri velit.** (Modestinus, D. 28. 1. 1.)

The forms of Wills have varied at different periods of Roman law.

I. Under the solemn forms of the old law they were made (always orally), 1, at the half-yearly *comitia calata*, or assembly of Patricians; 2, *in procinctu* (on going out to battle). *Uti legassit super pecunia tutelare suæ rei, ita jus esto.* (XII. Tables.) These forms were obsolete in the time of Gaius.

II. *Per æs et libram*, with copper and scales—a form of *mancipatio* or fictitious sale before five witnesses and a *libripens* who was originally the heir, but in the time of Gaius a stranger. (For a description of this ceremony, see Gai. II. 104, and *Ancient Law*, p. 205.)

* It is unnecessary to point out the falsity of Justinian's definition, "*quod testatio mentis est.*" *Frequentissimæ in jure derivationes satis contortæ sunt, quales Stoicis erant sollennes,* e.g., *testamentum, quasi mentis testatio; mutuum, ex meo fit tuum; peculium, quasi pusilla pecunia; divortium, quasi diversitas mentium: agnati, quasi a patre cognati.* (Heineccius.)

III. The prætorian law recognised wills *sealed* by seven witnesses without the solemn forms, by giving *bonorum possessio* (p. 135) to the heirs instituted.

IV. The imperial constitutions (after Theodosius II.) abolishing the old emblematic ceremonies established a new form, derived from the three sources of the civil law, the prætorian law, and imperial constitutions ("*tripartita*," of triple origin), which required, 1, unity of context, 2, the testator's signature attested by seven witnesses present at the same time, and 3, the seals and signatures of the witnesses.*

V. Justinian adds that the name of the heir must be written in the will by the testator or witnesses. (This formality is suppressed in the Novels.)

Wills may also be made orally in the presence of seven witnesses.

Soldiers on service, *propter nimiam imperitiam*, are released from formalities in expressing their last wishes, which need only be clear and capable

* "The New Testament thus described is the one generally known as the Roman Will. But it was the Will of the Eastern Empire only; and the researches of Savigny have shown that in Western Europe the old Mancipatory Testament, with all its apparatus of conveyance, copper and scales, continued to be the form in use far down in the Middle Ages." *Ancient Law*, p. 214.

of proof. Gaius says that they may make testaments *quomodo velint vel quomodo possint.* (II. 114.) But their informal wills are not valid for more than a year after their discharge. Many persons debarred from becoming heirs or legatees by the civil law may take under a military will. (Gai. II. 110.)

No one (except soldiers) can die partly testate and partly intestate. *Nemo paganus partim testatus, partim intestatus decedere potest.*

Witnesses must have the *testamenti factio* with the testators.

*Testamenti factio* is used to mean the legal power (1) of making, (2) of taking under, and (3) of witnessing, a will. In each case the possession of the *jus Quiritium*, or rights of citizenship,* is necessary. The condition resembles the *connubium* which must exist between parties to a legal marriage.

*Who may not be witnesses.* Women, slaves, *impuberes*, deaf or dumb persons, prodigals, infamous and worthless persons, madmen, persons under the power of the testator, the instituted heir, or anyone in his power, his father in whose power he is, or his brothers under the power of the same father.

* Heineccius distinguishes the *jus Quiritium* from the *jus civitatis*, referring private rights to the former and public to the latter.

But legatees and *fideicommissarii* may be witnesses, without losing their rights under a will.

As a general rule, every Roman citizen may make a will.

Those who are under power but possess *castrense* or *quasi-castrense peculium* may dispose of it by will in the ordinary form. In the time of Gaius, a woman under *tutela* could not make a valid will without the *auctoritas* of her tutor.

*Who may not make wills.* Persons under paternal power (ordinarily), or under puberty, slaves, madmen (except during lucid intervals), prodigals interdicted from controlling their affairs, deaf, dumb, or blind persons (except with certain forms), captives in the power of an enemy, *peregrini*, *deportati* and (formerly) *Latini Juniani* and *dedititii*.

*Disinherison of children.* I. By the old law, a testator who had (1) a son in his power must institute him as heir, or disinherit him *by name*: otherwise the will was void, even though the son died in the testator's life-time.* Daughters or grandchildren might be disinherited by the general clause *ceteri exheredes sunto*. The omission, however, to disinherit them did not make

* The school of the Sabinians supported this view, but the Proculians were of the contrary opinion. See Introduction, p. 8.

the will invalid, but only gave them the right to share the inheritance with the instituted heirs in equal proportions, if *sui heredes* (p. 104) were appointed, but if *extranei* were instituted, to the amount of one half. (Gai. II. 124.) (2) Posthumous children must be instituted or disinherited, and (3) those who became *sui heredes* of the testator after the making of the will; also (4) adopted children, while in the power of their adoptive father, but not if emancipated by him; and (5) *quasi-agnati*. (Gai. II. 138, see p. 100.)

II. By the prætorian law (1) a grandson must be instituted or disinherited *by name*; (2) the prætor would not overthrow a will in which a son had been passed over unless that son survived the testator; (3) emancipated children must be instituted as heirs or disinherited. The prætor carried his rules into effect by giving the *possessio bonorum contra tabulas* (an equitable possession of the property contrary to the terms of the will) to the persons aggrieved, leaving only the name of legal heirs to those instituted (see p. 136).

III. By the law of Justinian, all children, and all descendants in the male line, of *either sex*, born or posthumous, *sui heredes* or emancipated, must be instituted heirs or disinherited by name. A testator must institute or disinherit by name a child given in adoption to an *extraneus*, but not to an ascendant. But the adoptor, unless an ascendant, is not obliged to institute or disinherit the adopted child, whose rights of succession to his natural father remain unaltered by the adoption.

A soldier on service is exempted from this rule; so also a mother or maternal grandfather.

*The institution of an heir* is the designation of one whom the testator wishes to continue his *persona* or legal personality. Without this the will is void. *Velut caput et fundamentum intelligitur totius testamenti heredis institutio.* (Gai. II. 229.) Gaius (II. 117) gives the solemn form anciently required, but abolished by Constantine II. in A.D. 339.

*Who may be instituted.* A testator may institute one or more heirs, whether free or slaves, and either his own slaves or those of another, including those over whom he has only a *nuda proprietas*, another having the usufruct, or those of whom he is a co-proprietor. If his own slave, he enfranchises him by implication; * if another's, the slave takes the inheritance for his

* In the time of Gaius it was necessary that the gift of freedom should be formally declared together with the institution, *quia sine libertate institutio in persona ejus non constitit.* (Gai. II. 187.)

master's benefit, provided that the master has the *testamenti factio* with the testator: otherwise the institution is void. An heir may be instituted conditionally, but not to or from any particular time, for in that case the rule against partial testacy and partial intestacy might be violated. An impossible or an immoral condition is considered not to have been written (*pro supervacuo*), and does not invalidate the will.

*Who may not be instituted.* 1. *Peregrini* and *deportati*, and (formerly) *Latini Juniani* and *dedititii.* 2. Uncertain persons (up to the time of Justinian). 3. Corporate bodies and temples (without special exceptions), but Constantine allowed a church to be instituted. 4. Women were formerly excluded by the *Lex Voconia* (A.U.C. 585) from institution by a testator registered at more than 100,000 *asses.* But they could take the inheritance by *fideicommissum.* (Gai. II. 270.) 5. Parties to an incestuous marriage, or their offspring; second husbands or wives when there has been issue of the first marriage; and natural children when there has been legitimate issue. 6. Before Justinian unmarried persons (*cœlibes*) were prevented by the *Lex Julia*, and *orbi* (childless persons) lost half the inheritance by the *Lex Papia Poppæa.* (Gai. II. 286.)

*Division of the inheritance.* Generally divided into 12 fractions, * called *unciæ* (ounces), which are comprehended in the word *as* (pound weight); but the testator may create more or less *unciæ* to make up the *as*: *e.g.*, if a testator gives to A. 6 *unciæ*, to B. 5, and to C. 2, A. takes $\frac{6}{13}$, B. $\frac{5}{13}$, and C. $\frac{2}{13}$. Several heirs take equally unless otherwise specified. If each has his share specified and a residue remains unbequeathed, each takes of it in proportion to his share. So if the shares specified exceed the *as*, each heir suffers a diminution.

*Vulgaris substitutio.* Common substitution (*sub institutio*) is a subordinate institution of heirs in default of the original institution. One person may be substituted for several, or several for one, or the heirs themselves reciprocally. If one of several heirs does not take his share, it accrues to his co-heirs by the *jus accrescendi.*

*Pupillaris substitutio.* A testator having a child in his power, *under puberty*, may provide

* These fractions were known by the following names:—

| | | | |
|---|---|---|---|
| *Uncia* . . | = $\frac{1}{12}$ | *Septunx* . . | = $\frac{7}{12}$ |
| *Sextans* . . | = $\frac{2}{12}$ | *Bes* (*bistriens*) . | = $\frac{8}{12}$ |
| *Quadrans* . . | = $\frac{3}{12}$ | *Dodrans* . . | = $\frac{9}{12}$ |
| *Triens* . . . | = $\frac{4}{12}$ | *Dextans* . . | = $\frac{1}{12}$ |
| *Quincunx* . . | = $\frac{5}{12}$ | *Deunx* . . . | = $\frac{11}{12}$ |
| *Semis* . . . | = $\frac{\ }{12}$ | *As* . . . | = $\frac{1}{1}$ |

Hence, an inheritor of the whole estate is called *heres ex asse*, of half, *ex semisse*, &c.

that in case such child should succeed him as heir (and die under age, and therefore unable to make a valid will), some one else should be the child's heir. This amounts to the father making the child's will, but he must make one for himself at the same time. *Duo quodammodo sunt testamenta, aut certe unum est testamentum duarum hereditatum.* (Gaius.) He may also substitute to disinherited and posthumous children, but not to those whom he has emancipated.

This *substitutio* illustrates the well-known anxiety of the Romans to avoid an intestacy. In order to protect the pupil from *insidiæ* on the part of those interested in procuring an intestacy, the name of the substitute was written and sealed up in the concluding tablets of the will, which were not opened *vivo filio et adhuc impubere.*

A testator often makes a common and a pupillary substitution at the same time.

*Quasi-pupillaris substitutio.* By the law of Justinian a man having children or other descendants, of whatever sex or degree, who are *insane*, may substitute "certain persons" as heirs in their place, although they are not under puberty. The testator is limited in the first instance to descendants of the insane, or (if none) to brothers and sisters. If there are neither, his choice is unrestrained. The power is given to any ascendant, not being limited to children under *potestas*. But on the return of reason the substitution is void, as in pupillary substitution on the arrival of the age of puberty.

*Invalidation*. A will is, 1, *injustum, imperfectum ab initio*, if it does not comply with the formalities prescribed by law.

2. It is *ruptum* by the testator (i) cancelling or destroying it with that intention; (ii) making a new valid will (but if the second confirms the first, the first is regarded as a codicil); (iii) by the subsequent birth of a child passed over; (iv) by the testator, after the making of the will, arrogating a person *sui juris*, or adopting a child in the power of his natural father, or acquiring *manus* over his wife, or receiving back into his *potestas* a son manumitted after the first or second mancipation. Gaius (II. 140) says that as such *quasi-agnati* (being *extranei* at the time of making the will) could not have been instituted or disinherited in the character of *sui heredes*, it is superfluous to inquire whether they were named in the will or not. But this strict rule was afterwards relaxed, and the quasi-agnation of a person who had been instituted or disinherited did not invalidate the will.

3. It is *irritum* (ineffectual) when the testator

suffers a *capitis deminutio*,* and 4, *destitutum* when the inheritance is abandoned by the heir refusing or being unable to accept (but valid as to legacies and *fideicommissa*). But though invalid at civil law, a will is recognised by the prætorian system if sealed by seven witnesses (provided that the testator be a Roman citizen, and *sui juris*, at the time of his death), and the instituted heir may obtain *bonorum possessio secundum tabulas* (p. 136) from the prætor, either beneficially (*cum re*), if he can hold the inheritance against the legal heirs, or, if not, *sine re*. (Gai. II. 148.)

5. *Inofficiosum testamentum*, or unduteous will. Children (whether under power or not, born or adopted by an ascendant) unjustly disinherited have an action *de inofficioso testamento* (*i.e.*, *contra officium pietatis*, contrary to natural affection) against their parents, to recover one-fourth of the inheritance and *vice-versâ*. In cases where infamous persons have been instituted, the right is extended to the brothers and sisters of the testator, if *consanguinei*, formerly during agnation only, but under Justinian *durante agnatione vel non*.

The *querela*, or action for the *quarta legitima*,

* *Maxima enim servum faciebat, media peregrinum, minima filiumfamilias: quorum nullus testari poterat.* Heinec. *Antiq. Rom.* p. 439.

is not given to an arrogated son disinherited by the arrogator, because he has already the *quarta Antonina* (*vide* p. 51). It can only be successfully employed as a last resource. It is barred by the fourth having been given by hereditary right, legacy, *fideicommisum* or *donationes*. The fourth is divided proportionably among all the successful applicants, if more than one. If any portion has been given them under the will, they can only recover the balance of the fourth by an *actio in supplementum legitimæ*.

*The right to the action is lost*, 1, by death before showing an intention to claim it; 2, by delaying to claim it for five years; 3, by directly or indirectly approving the will.

Austin compares the French *légitime*, and observes that a similar law now obtains in probably every country in Europe except England (p. 638).

[*Changes made in the Novels.* The fourth is increased to half the inheritance where there are more than four claimants, otherwise to a third. The share cannot be given by legacy or *fideicommissum*. The claimants must have been instituted heirs; the proper reasons for disinherison are specified, and they are to be expressed in the will and proved by the instituted heir. If declared *inofficiosum*, the will is only rescinded as far as regards the institution of the heir, and the rest is good. The right is extended to *uterine* brothers and sisters.]

See Appendix (p. 213), and Maine's *Ancient Law*, c. 6.

## OF HEIRS.

Inst. II. 19; III. 1. Gai. II. 153—173; 185—190.

*Hereditas* * *est successio in universum jus quod testator habuit.*

Heirs are, 1, *necessarii*, 2, *sui et necessarii*, and 3, *extranei*.

1. *Necessary heirs* are slaves who are instituted heirs, for they cannot refuse the inheritance. Such heirs are generally appointed by an insolvent

* "Inheritance was a universal succession occurring at a death. The universal successor was Hæres or Heir. He stepped at once into all the rights and all the duties of the dead man. He was instantly clothed with his entire legal person; and I need scarcely add that the special character of the Hæres remained the same, whether he was named by a will or whether he took on an intestacy. . . . . But the Heir was not necessarily a single person. A group of persons considered in law as a single unit might succeed as co-heirs to the inheritance." "The notion was, that though the physical person of the deceased had perished, his legal personality survived and descended unimpaired on his Heir or Co-Heirs, in whom his identity (so far as the law was concerned) was continued. . . . . Unless provision was made in the will for the instant devolution of the testator's rights and duties on the Heir or Co-Heirs, the testament lost its effect." *Ancient Law*, p. 181.

that the ignominy of a *venditio bonorum* may attach to them rather than to the memory of the testator. They may apply to the prætor for the *beneficium separandi* or right of separating and keeping untouched by the creditors of the testator any debt due to them from him, or any property acquired by them otherwise than out of the estate. Gaius contrasts this with the general rule of law as to the after-acquired property of insolvents: *cum ceterorum hominum quorum bona venierint pro portione, si quid postea adquirunt, etiam sæpius eorum bona veniri solent.* (II. 155.) See p. 142.

Another *beneficium separandi* may also be given in case of the heir himself having debts, for the purpose of keeping his creditors distinct from those of the testator.

2. *Heredes sui et necessarii* are the children or direct descendants of a *paterfamilias*, born or adopted, who are in his *immediate* power at the time of his death, and become *sui juris* at that moment.

*Postumi quoque, qui, si vivo parente nati essent, in potestate ejus futuri forent, sui heredes sunt.*

So a son taken prisoner in his father's lifetime (and therefore no longer under his power), but restored after his death, *suus heres parenti efficitur: jus enim postliminii hoc facit* (see p. 43).

Gaius mentions that a wife *in manu*, and a

daughter-in-law in the *manus* of a son, being in the position of daughter and grand-daughter to the *paterfamilias* were considered to be his *suæ heredes*.

Gaius, followed by Justinian, says that heirs are called *sui, quia domestici heredes sunt, et vivo quoque parente quodammodo domini existimantur*, and *necessarii, quia omnimodo, sive velint sive nolint, tam ab intestato quam ex testamento heredes fiunt*. Papinian refers the term *sui* to their being in the *potestas* of their *paterfamilias*.

In succeeding to an intestate the *sui* become heirs at the moment when the inheritance is vacant, though they may not be aware of their rights, or even though they may be *furiosi;* and in the case of pupils there is no need for the *auctoritas* of the tutor. *Statim morte parentis quasi continuatur dominium.*

The prætor, however, allows them to abstain from the inheritance if they wish (*beneficium abstinendi*), but they do not thereby lose the character of heirs. *Semel heres, semper heres.* No application is necessary for this *beneficium*. It was formerly extended to a son *in causa mancipii*, although he was in the position of a slave, and therefore a *necessarius heres*. But if the *sui heredes* once deal with the property, they cannot relinquish the inheritance.

3. *Extranei heredes* are those not in the power of the testator at the time of his death. They may accept or reject the inheritance (only in its integrity), but if they accept they must have *testamenti factio* with the testator at the time (i) of his making the will, (ii) of the inheritance falling to them, and (iii) of their entering upon it. Like *sui heredes* who do not abstain, if they once accept they cannot afterwards renounce, except minors under twenty-six *(perfecta ætas)*, who may also obtain complete restitution from the prætor after having refused the inheritance. *Deliberandi potestas*, or liberty to consider whether they will accept or refuse the inheritance, is allowed to *extranei heredes* (not less than 100 days nor more than nine months, or by special favour a year).

*Cretio.* In the time of Gaius an heir might be instituted with *cretio*—a time fixed by the testator for his acceptance or refusal. *Ideo cretio appellata est quia cernere est quasi decernere et constituere.* (Gai. II. 164.) *Cretio* was (1) *vulgaris*, running from the time when the heir knew his rights and was able to act on them, *quibus sciet poteritque*, and (2) *continua*, or *certorum dierum*, in which the time was reckoned continuously from the day when the right accrued *etiam nescienti.* This institution *cum cretione* was abolished by the Emperors Arcadius and Honorius in A.D. 407. An inheritance not yet entered upon is said to be an *hereditas jacens*. *Bona vacantia* are the property of persons dying without successors.

By the *beneficium inventarii* Justinian allows heirs to enter on the inheritance without being liable for debts beyond the value of the estate, if they make an inventory of the property. An *extraneus* may enter on the inheritance (i) by doing some act as heir (*pro herede gerere*), or (ii) by the mere intention to be heir (*nudâ voluntate*). But he is immediately barred by following a contrary intention. By the old law, if appointed with *cretio*, he could alter such contrary intention within the time specified by the testator.

The *Lex Voconia* (A.U.C. 585), which prohibited the institution of women as heirs by any one returned as having 100,000 *asses*, was not in force in the time of Justinian.

## OF LEGACIES.

Inst. II. 20. Gai. II. 191—245.

*Legatum est donatio quædam a defuncto legata.* (Just.) Ulpian says, *Legatum est quod legis modo, id est imperative relinquitur; nam ea quæ precativo modo relinquuntur, fideicommissa vocantur.*

Legacies were formerly of four kinds, to each of which certain *formulæ* were attached: 1, *per vindicationem* (*Capito*, *Sumito*, or *Do*, *Lego*); 2, *per damnationem* (*Heres meus damnas esto dare, dato, facito*); 3, *sinendi modo* (*Heres meus damnas esto sinere Lucium sumere, &c.*); 4, *per præceptionem* (*Præcipito*).

Gaius explains fully the nature of these forms and the modes of recovering property left under each. 1. *Per vindicationem* was limited to property owned by the testator as *dominus ex jure Quiritium*, both at the time of making the will and at his death, (but at the latter time only in the case of *res fungibiles*). As soon as the heir had entered, the property bequeathed passed at once to the legatee, and he could recover by a *vindicatio* or real action. The Proculians held that the legatee must have the *intentio* to accept before the property could pass, and in the meantime it would be a *res nullius*, as (they thought) in the case of a legacy given subject to a condition, *pendente conditione.*

2. *Per damnationem.* This form constituted a mere charge against the heir, and did not pass a real right or *jus in rem.* The legatee could only recover, therefore, by a *condictio* or personal action. All kinds of property could be passed, even though belonging to another, or not yet in

existence (as fruits, or the young of animals). If the legacy were given to two or more persons *disjunctim*, each could claim the whole (or its value) from the heir—*singulis solida res debetur*—which was not the case in the preceding form.

3. *Sinendi modo.* In this way the testator charged the heir to suffer the legatee to take possession of the property bequeathed. The legatee could only recover by a *condictio.* The testator could bequeath anything belonging to himself or his heir at the time of his death, but not a *res aliena.*

4. *Per præceptionem.* Strictly, this kind of legacy was made to one of the instituted heirs, and could include nothing but the testator's own property. The Sabinians held that the legatee could only recover by the *actio familiæ erciscendæ* (suit to divide an inheritance), while the Proculians made the form equivalent to *per vindicationem* by reading the '*præ*' as superfluous.

By the *SC Neronianum* (A.D. 60) it was enacted *ut quod minus aptis verbis legatum est perinde sit ac si optimo jure legatum esset.* So that if a legacy were void under one form, it was held to be as valid as the widest and most favourable form (*per damnationem*) could make it.

Justinian abolishes these distinctions, making all legacies of the same nature, and placing them on the same footing as *fideicommissa* (see next title).

*Necessarium esse duximus omnia legata fideicommissis exæquare, ut nulla sit inter ea differentia; sed quod deest legatis, hoc repleatur ex natura fideicommissorum, et si quid amplius est in legatis, per hoc crescat fideicommissorum natura.* (Inst. II. 20. 3.)

*Objects and effects of legacies.* All things subject to commerce, corporeal or incorporeal, may be bequeathed. A testator may leave as a legacy the property of another, and if the legatee can prove that he knew it to be so, the heir must buy the object for the legatee or pay him the value. If a testator gives as a legacy a thing pledged to a creditor which he knew to be pledged, the heir must redeem it. If the legatee has acquired the thing left to him by way of clear gain (*causa lucrativa*) and without burden or expense, before he is entitled to it under the will, he cannot regain it or its value. Future products may be given as a legacy. If the same thing is bequeathed to two or more persons, either jointly or separately, they take equally; but if any fail to take, their shares go by accrual (*jus accrescendi*)* to the rest, unless the testator expressly forbids it. If a testator gives his own

The rules of the *jus accrescendi*, as applied to legacies, varied at different stages in the history of the law. 1. By the old law, if the legacy were given *per vindicationem* or *per præ-*

property as a legacy and then sells it (without intending to revoke the legacy), the legatee is entitled to it. So if a testator pledges immovables which he has given as a legacy. If a creditor gives a discharge to his debtor as a legacy (*legatum liberationis*) the heir cannot recover the debt from the debtor. A man may bequeath to his wife her marriage portion (*prælegare dotem*),* if he has received it. The *regula Catoniana* provided that a legacy invalid at the time of making the will could never become valid, *quod, si testamenti facti tempore decessisset testator, inutile foret, id legatum quandocunque decesserit non valere.*

*ceptionem* to more persons than one, either conjointly or separately, a lapsed portion (*portio deficientis*) accrued to the co-legatees. In conjoint legacies *per damnationem*, a *portio deficientis* lapsed to the inheritance. So in disjoint legacies, where the same thing was left under this form separately to more than one, as each co-legatee could claim from the heir the whole gift or its value, it was the inheritance which benefited by a lapse. 2. By the *Lex Papia Poppæa* (A.D. 10), legacies which lapsed either by force of the civil law (*in causâ caduci*), or by virtue of the *Lex*, were given (i) to co-legatees having children, (ii) to heirs who had children, (iii) to legatees generally having children, (iv) to the public treasury. The *Lex* did not apply to ascendants and descendants of the deceased, who enjoyed the *jus antiquum*. 3. Justinian abolishes the rules of the *Lex Papia* as to *caduca*, and restores the principles of the old law of legacies *per vindicationem*, without recognising the distinctions made under any other form.

* So called because the *dominium* of the *dos* remained in the wife, the husband taking only a life interest. The legacy would be more beneficial to the widow than an *actio de dote*.

*Quæ definitio,* Celsus adds, *in quibusdam falsa est.* (D. 34. 7. 1.) If the legacy perishes before delivery without the fault of the heir, the legatee loses it; otherwise, the heir is answerable.

The enfranchisement of a slave by will does not carry the gift of the *peculium,* unless expressly bequeathed. If it is given by legacy, an increase or diminution happening *in the lifetime of the testator* is at the gain or loss of the legatee; but when it takes place between the death of the testator and the entry of the heir (the *dies cedit* in this case) the legatee gains any augmentation derived *ex rebus peculiaribus,* but if *aliunde,* only if he be the slave himself and not an *extraneus.* When a slave has his *peculium* bequeathed to him, he cannot demand from the heir what he has expended *in rationes dominicas*—in the interest of his master.

The expression *dies cedit* (the day begins) applied to a legacy, means that the interest in it has vested, that the debt is owing; *dies venit* (the day is come), that it may be demanded for possession, that the debt is payable; the *dies cedit,* being the day of the testator's death (except in gifts of freedom to slaves and legacies of personal servitudes), and the *dies venit* the day of the heir's entry on the inheritance. The legatee takes the legacy just as it is on the *dies cedit.*

The legacy of a debt by a debtor to his creditor is valid, if it is of any advantage to the creditor.

*Legatum nominis* is the legacy of a debt due to the testator.

*Legatum generis* is the legacy of one thing not particularly specified out of a class, the choice resting with the legatee unless reserved to the heir.

*Legatum optionis* is the legacy of a right to choose an object from among certain others. By the old law, if the legatee died without making his choice, the legacy perished with him. Justinian allows his heirs to take if he survives the testator. When the choice is left to more than one, if the legatees cannot agree, the decision is made by lot.

Legatees must have *testamenti factio* with the testator, *i.e.*, they must have the *jus Quiritium*, and not be under any legal disability (as heretics). (See p. 93.)

Legacies to uncertain persons (if they can be discovered) are valid. In the time of Gaius, such legacies were void without a *certa demonstratio*.

Formerly, a legacy to a *postumus alienus* (*i.e.*, one who, if born in the life-time of the testator, would not have been in his power, and consequently not among his *sui heredes*) was void. Nor could he be instituted as heir, though the prætor gave him *bonorum possessio.* Justinian allows both, *nisi in utero ejus sit quæ jure nostro uxor esse non potest.*

A testator cannot give a legacy to the slave of his heir (except on the condition of his being free when the *dies cedit*), but if a slave be instituted heir, a legacy may be given to his master, provided that the slave has ceased to be in his power at the time of entering on the inheritance.

A mistake in the *nomen*, *prænomen*, or *cognomen* of a legatee, or a false description, or a false reason for giving the legacy, does not make it invalid.

A legacy written in the will before the institution of the heir, or made to take effect after the death of the heir or legatee, or given by way of penalty (*pœnæ nomine*) is made valid by Justinian. (Invalid by the old law.)

A legacy may be revoked or transferred in the same will or in a codicil. Also by disposal in the testator's lifetime.

See Appendix, p. 214.

## OF THE LEX FALCIDIA.

By the law of the XII. Tables, a testator was unrestricted in the disposal of his property, and might leave to his heir nothing but the empty name. The consequent abstention of heirs resulted in frequent intestacies, and legislation became necessary.

1. The *Lex Furia* (B.C. 182) limited individual legacies or donations *mortis causa* to sums of 1000 *asses*. 2. By the *Lex Voconia* (B.C. 169) no single legatee could take more than the heirs received. 3. As both these laws were evaded by the multiplication of legacies, the *Lex Falcidia* (B.C. 40) provided that no testator should give more than three-fourths of his property in legacies, so that one-fourth might always remain to the heir or heirs.

The value of the estate is taken at the testator's death, and the fourth calculated after deducting his debts, funeral expenses, and the price of the manumission of his slaves.

The heir cannot claim the benefit of the law unless he has made an inventory of the estate.

The law does not apply to military testaments.

The *Lex* was extended (1) by the *SC Pegasianum* to *fideicommissa;* (2) by Antoninus Pius to *fideicommissa* charged on successors *ab intestato;* (3) by Septimius Severus to donations *mortis causa;* and (4) to gifts between husband and wife.

In the Novels, Justinian allows the testator to exclude the operation of the *Lex* by a special declaration.

## OF FIDEICOMMISSA.

Inst. II. 23, 24. Gai. II. 246—289.

*Fideicommissa* are gifts in trust, 1, of the whole inheritance, and 2, of a particular thing. They are generally testamentary, but may also be made by an intestate on his death-bed. They were originally invented to enable a testator to bequeath property to a person with whom he had not the *testamenti factio*, through the medium of some one who was capable of taking, in trust for the beneficiary (*fideicommissarius*). At first the heir (*fiduciarius*) was only bound in honour to execute the trust, but it was afterwards enforced by the consuls (under Augustus), and finally by a special *prætor fideicommissarius*. *Fideicommissa* are not subject to the strict rules of the civil law as to legacies, and may be expressed in any language. All kinds of property may be passed by them to almost any beneficiaries irrespectively of *testa-*

*menti factio*, and they may be simple or conditional.

An heir must be appointed in a will containing a *fideicommissum*.

Gaius says that when the heir has given up the inheritance to the *fideicommissarius*, he still remains heir, but the beneficiary stands sometimes *heredis loco*, sometimes *legatarii*. Formerly, *nec heredis loco erat nec legatarii, sed potius emptoris*, for the inheritance was sold *nummo uno dicis causa* to the beneficiary, who undertook by *stipulationes emptæ et venditæ hereditatis* to indemnify the heir against all losses and expenses on account of the inheritance, while the heir promised to give up whatever might accrue to the estate, and to allow the *fideicommissarius* to conduct *hereditarias actiones* as his agent (*procurator* or *cognitor*).

By the *SC Trebellianum* (A.D. 62) the *fideicommissarius* took the place of the heir at once, without the old fiction of sale, the prætor granting *utiles actiones* (p. 169) to and against him, instead of the heir.

If the heir was called upon to give up more than three-fourths of the estate, the *SC Pegasianum* (A.D. 70), without repealing the former *SC*, allowed him to retain a Falcidian fourth, as if he took no benefit he might refuse the inheritance, and the trust would perish. When the heir took a fourth, he and the beneficiary made stipulations *partis et pro parte* as to sharing the benefits and burdens of the inheritance in proportion to their respective interests. Thus the beneficiary was placed *legatarii partiarii loco*, for he shared the inheritance with the heir. If the heir did not choose to take a fourth, he and the beneficiary made the stipulations *emptæ et venditæ hereditatis* above mentioned. If the heir refused the inheritance, the prætor could, at the request of the beneficiary, order him to enter and give it up, at the same time granting *utiles actiones* to and against the recipient as under the *SC Trebellianum*. In this case there was no need of any stipulations, as the heir could neither gain nor lose by the inheritance. *Qui jussu prætoris adit hereditatem, omni commodo prohiberi debet.* (Julian, D. 36. 27. 14.)

Justinian unites these two *SCC* into one, under the name of *SC Trebellianum*, by which the heir retains the fourth or deducts a particular thing as an equivalent, and the beneficiary stands *in loco heredis.* If the heir is requested to give up the inheritance after retaining a fourth, the actions are proportionably divided between him the *fideicommissarius* (*scinduntur actiones*). So if the heir has to retain a part of the inheritance to supplement a legacy worth less than a fourth, as far as relates to that part. But if he deducts a particular thing as an equivalant, the actions are transferred to the beneficiary *in solidum.*

A legacy to the heir, equal in value to not less than a fourth of the inheritance, is considered as a satisfaction of the fourth given by the new *SC Trebellianum*, and he takes it free from incumbrance as a simple legatee. The whole residue of the inheritance, with its rights and obligations, is then transferred to the beneficiary.

A beneficiary may be charged with a further *fideicommissum*, but may not retain a fourth like the heir. He may put the heir to his oath to say whether he has been charged with a trust or not.

A person about to die intestate may charge his successors (whether *heredes legitimi* or *bonorum possessores*) with a *fideicommissum.*

Particular things may be left by *fideicommissum*, whether the property of the testator, the heir, a legatee, or any one else. *Hoc solum observandum est*, says Gaius, *ne plus quisquam rogetur alicui restituere quam ipse ceperit.*

A testator may enfranchise his own slave, or another's, by *fideicommissum.* A slave so enfranchised becomes the freedman of the *fiduciarius* who manumits him; but if enfranchised directly by will, *ipsius testatoris libertus fit, qui etiam Orcinus appellatur.* (See p. 39.)

A *fideicommissum* is generally expressed by the words *peto, rogo, volo, mando,* or *tuæ fidei committo.*

Gaius enumerates the difference between *fideicommissa* and legacies existing (1) before his time, and (2) at the period in which he wrote.

1. Formerly (1) *peregrini* could take *fideicommissa* (up to the time of Hadrian); also (2) *cœlibes* and *orbi* (till the *SC Pegasianum*, A.D. 70); so, too (3), uncertain persons and *postumi alieni* (till the time of Hadrian); and (4) *fideicommissa* could probably be made *pœnæ nomine.*

2. In the time of Gaius, unlike a legacy (1) a *fideicommissum* could be given by a nod; (2) it could be charged on *heredes ab intestato;* (3) it could be contained in unconfirmed codicils; (4) it could be charged on a legatee or a first *fideicommissarius;* (5) it could confer liberty on another man's slave; (6) it could charge an heir, even in an unconfirmed codicil (see p. 123), to give up the whole or part of an inheritance; (7) it could pass an inheritance to a woman contrary to the terms of the *Lex Voconia;* (8) it could pass inheritances or legacies to *Latini* (contrary to the *Lex Junia*); (9) contrary to a *SC*, it enabled a slave less than thirty years old to be instituted heir and enfranchised, and on reaching that age to claim his liberty and

the inheritance; (10) it could charge an heir on the day of his death (*cum morietur*) to give up the inheritance in whole or part to another; (11) it could be given after the death of the heir; (12) it must be recovered before the consul or *prætor fideicommissarius*, or governor of a province, and not by means of a *formula* (as a legacy) *per ordinarium judicium;* (13) it could be recovered at Rome throughout the year, and not (like legacies) only on days appointed for legal business,* *cum res aguntur;*

* In the time of Gaius there were 230 such days in the year.

*Ille Nefastus erit, per quem Tria Verba* (*do, dico, addico*) *silentur;*
*Fastus erit, per quem lege licebit agi.*—Ovid, *Fasti*, I. 47.

On the introduction of Christianity, the old holidays (*feriæ*) were superseded by the Sunday and Christian festivals. A constitution of Valentinian II., Theodosius I., and Arcadius, in A.D. 389 (the era of the formal extinction of paganism), while declaring all days to be *juridici*, directs two months to be observed as holidays in summer and autumn, also Sundays, the foundation-days of Rome and Constantinople, the first of January, and a week at each of the festivals of Christmas, Epiphany, and Easter. From a constitution of Theodosius I., it appears that the harvest and vintage vacations extended from the 8th of July to the 1st of August and from the 10th of September to the 15th of October. Another constitution orders all criminal proceedings to be suspended during Lent (Cod. 3. 12. 2. and 7). In England, it was directed by Edward the Confessor "that from advent to the octave of the epiphany, from the ascension to the octave of pentecost, and from three in the afternoon of all Saturdays till Monday morning, the peace of God and of holy church shall be kept throughout all the kingdom." "And so extravagant," says Blackstone, "was afterwards the regard that

(14) it carried interest and accumulations in case of delay; (15) it was valid though written in Greek; (16) *fideicommissi nomine semper in simplum persecutio est*, but in a legacy *per damnationem* an action lay against the heir for double; (17) *quod quisque ex fideicommisso plus debito per errorem solverit, repetere potest*, but not so in a legacy *per damnationem*, nor when a legacy has been paid which is not due; (18) although *fideicommissa* were generally of much wider scope than legacies, a tutor could be appointed by the latter, but not by the former.

As already stated, Justinian places legacies on an equality with *fideicommissa* (Inst. II. 20. 3.), but the distinction as to the gift of liberty to the slave of another (5) remains in force.

See Appendix, p. 215.

was paid to these holy times, that in the reign of king Edward I. (till the Stat. of Westminster 1) no secular plea could be held, nor any man sworn on the evangelists, in the times of advent, lent, pentecost, harvest and vintage, the days of the great litanies, and all solemn festivals." The portions of time not included in these prohibited seasons produced the fourfold division of Hilary, Easter, Trinity, and Michaelmas Terms. These periods have since been regulated by several Acts of Parliament, and the Easter and Trinity Terms no longer depend upon the movable feasts from which they take their name and origin. See Blackstone, vol. III. p. 275.

## OF CODICILS.

### Inst. II. 25. Gai. II. 270, 273.

Codicils were not in use before Augustus. They were invented by the jurists. If unattached to a will, they are directions to the *heredes ab intestato.* If confirmed by subsequent will, they are considered to form part of it. If subsequent to the will, they need not be confirmed. They may create *fideicommissa* without a will. Their number is unlimited, but whether verbal or in writing, they must be made *uno contextu*, and before five witnesses, who must sign them if written. They need not be written or signed by the testator.

An heir can neither be instituted nor disinherited, nor can an institution be revoked, nor substitution made, by codicils (even though confirmed by will) except through a *fideicommissum.*

## OF INTESTATE SUCCESSION.

### Inst. III. 1—6. Gai. III. 1—24.

An intestate is one who dies without a will, or who leaves a will which is revoked, invalid, or abandoned by the heir.

By the law of the XII. Tables the inheritance of an intestate devolved on, 1, his *sui heredes*,

2, the *agnati*, and 3, the *gentiles** (afterwards of the *cognati*, by prætorian law).

1. *Sui heredes* (*vide* p. 104). The *sui* called to the inheritance are those who are in the *immediate* power of the deceased at the time of his death, and who become *sui juris* at that moment. Therefore, if the intestate has a son and a grandson by that son both in his power, the son succeeds, and not the grandson. Those permitted to rank with the *sui* are not *necessarii heredes*. Among *sui heredes* inheritances are divided *per stirpes* (by representation), and not *per capita* (in equal shares to all in their own right), as among *agnati* and *cognati*, so that grandchildren take the share of their deceased parent, and the nearer in degree do not exclude the more remote.

*The prætorian law.* Although emancipated children cannot be *sui heredes*, the prætor *naturali*

* The *gentiles* were "the collective members of the dead man's *gens* or House. The house was a fictitious extension of the family, consisting of all Roman Patrician citizens who bore the same name, and who, on the ground of bearing the same name, were supposed to be descended from a common ancestor. Now the Patrician Assembly, called the *Comitia Curiata*, was a Legislature in which *gentes* or Houses were exclusively represented. It was a representative assembly of the Roman people, constituted on the assumption that the constituent unit of the state was the *Gens*." (*Ancient Law*, p. 200.) *Plebs gentem non habet.* Cicero says, *Gentiles sunt qui inter se eodem nomine sunt, qui ab ingenuis oriundi, quorum majorum nemo servitutem serviit, qui capite non sunt deminuti.*

*æquitate motus* gives them the *possessio bonorum unde liberi* (p. 136) for their share of the inheritance. But they must bring into the inheritance all the property they possessed at the time of the father's death (*collatio bonorum*), because if they had remained in the family they would have acquired it for him. Besides emancipated children, if they themselves are dead, their children conceived after the emancipation have the *possessio bonorum*.

When a will does not expressly disinherit a *suus heres*, or one who has been raised to that rank, the prætor gives him *possessio bonorum contra tabulas*, the same rules applying as to emancipated children.

Formerly an adopted son who remained in his adoptive family lost his right of succession to his natural father, but became a *suus heres* of his adoptive father. If emancipated by his adoptive father in the lifetime of his natural father, the prætor gave him the succession to his natural father, but he lost all claims as a *suus heres* on his adoptive father. If he left his adoptive family after his natural father's death, he lost all claims on either father, except to *bonorum possessio* as a *cognatus* of his natural father in default of *sui heredes* and *agnati*.

By a constitution of Justinian, children adopted

by an *extraneus* do not lose their right of succeeding to the inheritance of their natural father as *sui heredes*, while they gain the right of succeeding *ab intestato* to their adoptive father. But an adoptive father is in no way bound to institute or disinherit an adopted son. This does not apply to children adopted by an ascendant (*adoptio plena*).

Formerly grandchildren by a daughter were not allowed to rank as *sui heredes*, but by imperial constitutions they could succeed to two-thirds of their mother's share, if there were other *sui heredes*, and to three-fourths if there were only *agnati* to come in with the mother. Justinian allows them to take the whole of her share. They are, however, necessarily *extranei heredes*.

2. *Legitima agnatorum hereditas.* In default of *sui heredes* and those who rank with them the law calls the nearest *agnati*, or *legitimæ personæ, i.e.*, relatives (both male and female), by unbroken *male* descent from a common ancestor, and members of the same civil family (p. 58). By the law of the XII Tables *only the nearest* agnate or degree of agnates could succeed before the *gentiles*: so that if the nearest agnates refused the inheritance or died before entering, the succession passing over the remaining agnates devolved on the *gentiles*. But Justinian allows all the *agnati* of whatever

degree according to proximity to take before the *cognati*, the nearest degree excluding the more remote. Gaius remarks that in his time the prætorian law had corrected this and other inequalities of the civil law by calling to the inheritance *omnes qui legitimo jure deficiuntur.* This illustrates the *levelling* character of Roman equity. (See *Anc. Law*, p. 58.)

The XII Tables made no distinction between male and female *agnati*, but the *responsa prudentum*, which formed the *media jurisprudentia* prior to the imperial constitutions, *subtilitate quadam excogitatâ* expressly excluded women beyond the degree of sisters (*consanguineæ* or *germanæ*) from the succession of *agnati.** The prætors gave them *bonorum possessio unde cognati* if there were no *agnati*, but Justinian restores the law of the XII Tables.

*Agnatio* was destroyed by *capitis deminutio.* Therefore emancipated children lost the rights of agnation. But the Emperor Anastasius (503 A.D.) allowed emancipated brothers and sisters to succeed as agnates to one half of their natural share. Justinian gives them their whole share, and admits their children, together with uterine brothers and sisters and their children. But the

* *Id, jure civili, Voconionâ ratione videtur effectum* (Paul.)

inheritance is divided *per capita*, and not *per stirpes* (as among *sui heredes*), so that if the intestate leaves a brother or sister, and they accept the inheritance, the more remote degrees are ex cluded.

The time for ascertaining the nearest *agnati* is at the death of the intestate; or if the deceased has made a will, as soon as it is certain that there will be no testamentary heir.

An ascendant who has emancipated a descendant may succeed to his property under an implied fiduciary contract next after the brothers and sisters of the deceased.

*Germani* are children by the same father and mother, *consanguinei* by the same father but not the same mother, *uterini* by the same mother but not the same father. *Consanguineus* is often used as equivalent to *germanus*.

By the old law there was no succession between mother and child, but the prætor gave them *bonorum possessio unde cognati* (p. 136).

The *SC Tertullianum* (158 A.D.) permitted a mother who had three children (if a freedwoman, four) to succeed in the rank of *agnati* to her son or daughter *dying without issue*, though not to any further descendants. But she was excluded by any brothers (*consanguinei*) of her deceased child; or if there were no brothers, but sisters, by the same father, she took an equal half with them. The *jus trium liberorum* only availed as an excuse from serving the office of tutor (p. 65) and other duties, if the children were alive or had died in war (*qui pro republica ceciderunt, in perpetuum, per gloriam, vivere intelliguntur*). One of the penalties of celibacy imposed by the *Lex Papia Poppæa* was the inability to take under a will, so in order to enable their temples to receive legacies, the Gods themselves, and even the Vestal Virgins, had the honour of three children ascribed to them. The privilege was also sold by the emperors. Paul says: *Jus liberorum mater habet, quæ tres liberos aut habet, aut habuit, aut neque habet neque habuit. Habet cui supersunt. Habuit quæ amisit. Neque habet neque habuit, quæ beneficio principis jus liberorum consecuta est.* (*Sent.* IV. 9.) But it was not necessary for this purpose that the children should be surviving.

Justinian allows a mother to succeed irrespectively of the number of her children. If there are sisters only of deceased, the mother takes half and the sisters the other half. If there are brothers only, or both brothers and sisters (whether *consanguinei* or *uterini*), the mother takes equally with them *per capita*. The right does not extend to the grandmother. In the case of children dying *impuberes*, a mother might lose her succession by having neglected to obtain a tutor for them during the space of a year. The *SC* applies to illegitimate children.

The *SC Orphitianum* (178 A.D.) permits children to succeed to their mothers dying intestate. They are preferred to the *consanguinei*, or *agnati* in the second degree (*i.e.*, brothers and sisters natural or adopted), or to any more remote *agnati*.

Imperial constitutions extend this right to grandchildren. It is lost by *capitis deminutio maxima* and *minor*, but not *minima*. This *SC* also applies to illegitimate children.

*Accrual.* When there are several *heredes legitimi*, and any fail to take their shares, such shares accrue to those who accept the inheritance; and if any who have entered die before the accrual, then to their heirs. But by a constitution of Justinian the share of an heir who dies while exercising the *jus deliberandi* passes to his own heirs, and does not accrue.

3. *Cognatorum successio.* In default of *sui heredes*, *agnati*, and those permitted to rank with either, the prætor calls the nearest *cognati* to succeed (instead of the *gentiles* of the XII Tables).

*Cognati* include all blood relations, male or female, descended from two legally married persons.

In this third order the prætor admits, 1, *agnati* who have lost the right of agnation by a *capitis deminutio minima; propter æquitatem rescindit eorum capitis deminutionem prætor* (Paul); 2, persons related collaterally only by the female line; 3, children in an adoptive family to the inheritance of their natural parents (see p. 51); 4, a mother to her children, and children to their mother; 5, female agnates beyond the degree of *consanguineæ** (Gai. III. 29); and 6, illegitimate children.

The changes of Justinian already noticed embodied much of the prætorian dispensation. The succession of *cognati* is limited to the sixth degree (except children of a second cousin in the seventh), while *agnati* may succeed beyond the tenth.

For calculating the degrees of collateral relationship, *vide sup.* p. 46.

*Servilis cognatio* was not recognised by the old law. But Justinian allows the offspring of a free parent and a slave, when both the slave parent and the children are enfranchised, to succeed to their parents, and bar the right of the patron (*patronatus jure in hac parte sopito*). Such children can also succeed to each other, *ad similitudinem eorum*

* *Feminæ ad hereditates legitimas ultra consanguineas successiones non admittuntur.* (Paul, *Sent. Rec.* IV. 8). See p. 127.

*qui ex justis nuptiis procreati sunt*, whether all born slaves or some free and others slaves, and whether born of the same father and mother, or only of the same father or the same mother.

For the changes made in the Novels, see p. 138.

The Roman law of Testamentary and Intestate succession is the model of almost all European law on those subjects. The English law of Wills differs from the Roman, but the Statute of Distributions is borrowed from the 118th and 127th Novels of Justinian.

See Appendix, p. 211; and *Ancient Law*, c. 7.

## OF THE SUCCESSION OF LIBERTI.

Inst. III. 7, 8. Gai. III. 39—76.

1. By the law of the XII Tables, a freedman might omit his patron in his will; a freedwoman could not make a will without the *auctoritas* of her patron, who was her *tutor legitimus*. If a freedman died intestate, the patron succeeded after the *sui heredes* (who might be gained by adoption). A freedwoman could have no *sui heredes*.

2. By the prætorian law, if a freedman had children born in marriage (whether in his power or not at the time of his death), and instituted them as heirs in his will, the patron was ex-

cluded. So if they were omitted, and obtained *bonorum possessio contra tabulas;* but not if disinherited, *nam exheredati nullo modo repellebant patronum.* If he had no *naturales liberi*, he must leave to his *patronus* (but not to a *patrona*), one half of his property. If he died intestate, his *sui heredes*, if gained only by adoption or marriage *in manu*, did not exclude the patron. The prætorian law did not alter the position of the *liberta*.

3. By the *Lex Papia Poppæa* (A.D. 10) increased rights were given to *patroni* in the case of rich *liberti*, whether dying testate or intestate, who left less than three children. If the freedman left 100,000 sesterces and two children, the patron took a third; if only one child, a half. A *liberta* who left four children was freed from the *tutela* of her patron; but if she made a will, he was entitled to a *pars virilis* or proportional share, according to the number of children that survived her. If she died intestate, the patron took the whole until the *SC Orphitianum* (p. 130), which excluded him in favour of her children.

If the patron died before the freedman, 1, by the law of the XII Tables, the patron's children and grandchildren *ex filio* of either sex succeeded to his right. 2. The prætorian law excluded the females. 3. For the provisions of the *Lex Papia*

*Poppæa*, see Gai. III. 45—54; and for the succession of patrons to *Latini Juniani* and *dediticii*, see Gai. III. 55—70, and Inst. III. 7. 4.

4. In the time of Justinian the following changes appear:—The distinction between *cives* and *Latini*, *patroni* and *patronæ*, *liberti* and *libertæ*, is abolished; if the freedman dies intestate, his children succeed first (see *servilis cognatio*, p. 131); in default of children, the patron and his descendants; and in default of these, the collaterals of the patron to the fifth degree. If the freedman has children, or leaves less than 100 *aurei* (one *aureus* being = 1000 sesterces), he may make what will he pleases; if no children, or if more than 100 *aurei*, he must leave his patron one-third, or the prætor will give it *contra tabulas*. *Pene enim consonantia jura ingenuitatis et libertinitatis in successionibus fecimus.* (Inst. III. 7. 3.).

*Assignatio libertorum.* If a freedman dies without children after the decease of his patron, his property devolves on all the children or descendants of the patron who are in the same degree. But the patron may assign a freedman or freedwoman to any one of his children of either sex, who will exclude the others. The right, however, is limited to a patron who has at least two children in his power, and he can only assign to children who are under his *potestas*.

The assignment may be made in any terms either with or without a will or codicil, and even by a nod. It may be as easily revoked, *etiam nudâ voluntate.*

### OF BONORUM POSSESSIO.

Inst. III. 9. Gai. III. 25—38.

*Bonorum possessio* is the succession to the aggregate of rights (*universitas rerum*) both of testators and intestates given by the prætorian law to persons who have not the character of heirs by the strict terms of the civil law. Ulpian defines it as the *jus persequendi retinendique patrimonii sive rei quæ cujusque cum moritur fuit.* The prætor's action takes place *confirmandi vel supplendi vel emendandi veteris juris gratiâ.* He cannot give immediate *dominium Quiritarium*, but only *bonitarium*, or equitable ownership,* nor can he admit anyone expressly excluded by the law. He some-

* But this *dominium bonitarium* may be ripened into *Quiritarium*, or complete legal ownership, by the operation of *usucapio* (p. 80). "The principal qualities of Roman property were incommunicable except through processes which were supposed to be co-eval with the origin of the Civil Law. The prætor therefore could not confer an Inheritance on any body. He could not place the Heir or Co-heirs in that very relation in which the Testator had himself stood to his own rights and obligations. All he could do was to confer on the person desig-

times confirms the law by giving *possessio secundum tabulas* (according to the terms of the faulty will), and also calls *sui heredes*, *agnati*, and *cognati* to the *possessio ab intestato*. The prætor cannot make a *legal* heir, but only a *bonorum possessor*, and he grants the *possessio* to many orders of persons from the wish that no one should die without a successor: in the case of testators, 1, *contra tabulas*, to children passed over in the will; 2, *secundum tabulas*, to the legally instituted heir, though the will is informal: in the case of intestates, 1, *possessio unde liberi*, to *sui heredes*, and those admitted to their rank, as emancipated children; 2, *unde legitimi*, to the legal heirs; 3, *unde decem personæ*, to the ten persons preferred to a *manumissor extraneus* (p. 53); 4, *unde cognati*, to the nearest *cognati* (see p. 130); 5, *tum quem ex familia*, to the nearest member of the family of the patron; 6, *unde patronus patronave*, to the patron or patroness, their children and ascendants: 7, *unde vir et uxor*, reciprocal rights of succession to a husband and wife, when the latter has not passed *in manum viri;* 8, *unde cognati manumissoris*, to the *cognati* of the *manu-*

nated as Heir the practical enjoyment of the property bequeathed, and to give the force of legal acquittance to his payments of the Testator's debts." *Ancient Law*, p. 211. *Apud peregrinos*, says Gaius, *unum est dominium*. II. 40. See p. 68.

*missor.* In default of all these, the *possessio* goes to the *fiscus* or imperial treasury as the *ultimus heres.*

Justinian abolishes the 3rd, 5th, 6th, and 8th, because he allowed parents who have emancipated their children to succeed to them by an implied fiduciary contract (p. 53), and because the successions of *libertini* and *ingenui* are now the same, except that those of the former are limited to the fifth degree. But he adds another *bonorum possessio*, called *uti ex legibus, viz.*, to those to whom it is given *ex novo jure* by any law, *SC*, or constitution, either in the case of testates or intestates. The prætor does not make it a settled rule, but uses it as a last and extraordinary resource, according to the exigencies of the case.

*Bonorum possessio* is said to be (1) *edictalis*, when the case falls under the general and formal orders of the Edict; and (2) *decretalis*, when only accorded after special consideration and under peculiar circumstances, perhaps with conditions and restrictions.

Gaius says that *bonorum possessio* might be given either (1) *cum re, i.e.*, beneficially, or (2) *sine re;* (1) *cum re*, if the *possessor* is assured of holding the *bona* with undisturbed possession against the legal heirs (*si nemo sit alius jure civili heres, ipsi retinere hereditatem possunt*); (2) *sine re*, if he is exposed to dispossession by the heirs at civil law. Com. II. 148, 149, and III. 35.

In the time of Justinian it was probably never given *sine re*. *Cum paulatim tam ex usu hominum quam ex constitutionum emendationibus, cœpit in unam consonantiam jus civile et prætorium jungi.* (Inst. II. 10. 3.)

Parents and children must demand the *possessio* within one year, all other persons within 100 *dies utiles*, *i.e.*, after they are aware of their right, otherwise those next in succession become entitled. Imperial constitutions allowed a mere expression of the wish to succeed to take the place of a formal demand.

[The system of intestate succession is completely changed by the 118th and 127th Novels (543 and 547 A.D.). The distinction between *hereditas* and *bonorum possessio, agnati* and *cognati*, males and females, is abolished. New order of succession: 1, descendants (emancipated or not, natural or adoptive, and whether descended through males or females), taking *per capita* in the first degree, and *per stirpes* in the second; 2, ascendants (the nearest excluding the more remote, and the paternal and maternal line each taking half). If there are no brothers or sisters of deceased of the whole blood, the ascendants take *per stirpes;* if there are, they take equally with the nearest ascendants *per capita;* 3, if there are neither descendants nor ascendants, then brothers and sisters of the whole blood, and in default of these, of the half blood. By the 127th Novel, children, but not grandchildren, of a deceased brother or sister, are admitted to represent their parent. 4. In default of brothers and sisters and their children, the nearest relation or degree of relations succeed (*per capita*, if more than one in same degree). In consequence of these changes, the *tutela legitima* (*vide* p. 58) falls to the nearest male relative of the deceased instead of the *agnati.*]

## OTHER MODES OF UNIVERSAL SUCCESSION.

Inst. III. 10—12. Gai. III. 77—87.

*Acquisitio per arrogationem.* In the time of Gaius, if a person gave himself in arrogation, all his property was acquired by the arrogator, except those things which were lost by the *capitis deminutio* (as usufruct, the right to the services of freedmen, &c.). By Justinian's law, if a *paterfamilias* gives himself in arrogation only, the usufruct of his property which is gained *extrinsecus* passes to the arrogator, who also succeeds to his rights of action for debt. But the arrogator is not liable for the son's debts, though he may be sued in his name by a *utilis actio* (p. 169); and if he does not defend him, the creditors may sell the son's property. In Justinian's time, use and usufruct were no longer lost by a change of *status familiæ.*

*Addictio bonorum libertatis causâ.* By a constitution of Marcus Aurelius, if an inheritance is successively refused by the *heredes ex testamento*, the *heredes ab intestato*, and the *fiscus*, and the testator has enfranchised slaves by his will, they may apply to have the property adjudged to them, instead of being sold by the creditors, in order to carry out the terms of the will, security being given for the full payment of the debts. So also if a master dies intestate, having enfranchised his slaves, when it is certain that no one will accept the inheritance.

If an heir who has renounced or abstained from the inheritance is *restitutus in integrum* after the *addictio* has taken place, the slaves do not thereby lose the liberty which they have once gained.

The *addictio* may also be given to slaves enfranchised *inter vivos* or *mortis causâ* to prevent defrauded creditors from applying to have the *manumissio* set aside under the *Lex Ælia Sentia.*

The *addictio* was afterwards extended to an *extraneus* (*i.e.* other than the slaves enfranchised), and Justinian allows it to take place even after the property of the deceased has been sold by creditors, *intra annale tamen tempus*. The creditors may also accept a dividend instead of taking security for full payment of the debts.

In the first Novel Justinian provides that if any instituted heir fail to carry out the dispositions of the will, the beneficiaries, or the heirs *ab intestato*, or even the *fiscus* may take his place, having first given security.

*Bonorum emptio per venditionem.* Gaius describes this form of succession *per universitatem*, but it disappeared with the *ordinaria judicia* (p. 175) more than 200 years before Justinian. It was a prætorian extension of the *bonorum sectio* of the civil law which gave the purchaser of an insolvent's estate sold by public auction, a *legal* succession (as of an heir) to all his rights (*in universum jus*). In *bonorum venditio* the goods sold might be (1), *vivorum;* and (2), *mortuorum*. 1, *vivorum*, in the case of fraudulent or absent insolvents, or of one who had made a voluntary surrender of his estate (*cessio bonorum ex lege Julia*)*, or of a judgment debtor against whom the allotted time had run.

* It appears from the Theodosian Code that *bonorum cessio* was confined by the *Lex Julia* to Roman citizens, but that it was extended to the provinces before the time of Diocletian. *C. Theod.* Tit. *Qui bon. ex. L. Jul. ced. possunt,* Laws 1 and 4.

2, *mortuorum*, in the case of those who have no heirs, *bonorum possessores*, or any other legal successors. The prætor gave the creditors possession of the property for thirty days in the first case and fifteen in the second, at the end of which a *magister* was appointed from among them to sell the estate in one lot after advertisement (*proscriptio*), and intervals of thirty and twenty days respectively. The *bonorum emptor* then stepped into the *universum jus* of the debtor or deceased, but (like a *bonorum possessor*) as he had only a prætorian title, his property was *in bonis* or *bonitarium*, but could be ripened into *dominium Quiritarium* by usucapion.

In Justinian's time, the property of insolvent debtors, instead of being sold in one lot, was disposed of in single or separate objects (*distractio bonorum*), the creditors dealing with them *prout utile eis visum fuerit.* Under this system the creditors had no claim on property acquired after the bankruptcy as they had in the time of Gaius (p. 104).

By the *SC Claudianum* if a free woman cohabited with a slave against the consent of his master, she lost both her property and her liberty to the master of the slave on account of her disgrace. If it was done with the master's knowledge, she did not become his slave, but was considered to be *libertinæ conditionis.* (Gai. I. 84, 91, 160.) Justinian abolishes this as being a *miserabilis per universitatem acquisitio.*

# BOOK III.—OF OBLIGATIONS.

## EX CONTRACTU AND QUASI EX CONTRACTU.

### Inst. III. 13—29. Gai. III. 88—181.

*Obligatio est juris vinculum* quo necessitate astringimur alicujus solvendæ rei secundum nostræ civitatis jura.*

Obligations are I. Civil; and II. Prætorian; according to the origin of the action which supports them.

They arise, I. *Ex contractu;* II. *Quasi ex contractu;* III. *Ex delicto;* and IV. *Quasi ex delicto.* Gaius does not make the divisions II. and IV., but he adverts to *quasi*-contracts (III. 91).

A *nudum pactum* is a convention or agreement, unclothed with an obligation, or any rights of action. *Quum nulla subest causa propter conventionem hic constat non posse constitui obligationem.* (D. 2. 14. 7.)

* "The image of a *vinculum juris* colours and pervades every part of the Roman law of Contract and Delict. The law bound the parties together, and the *chain* could only be undone by the process called *solutio*, an expression still figurative, to which our word 'payment' is only occasionally and incidentally equivalent." *Ancient Law*, p. 324.

An obligation is a right availing against a single individual or a group. *Obligationum enim substantia non in eo consistit ut aliquid nostrum faciat, sed ut alium nobis obstringat ad dandum aliquid, vel faciendum, vel præstandum.* As a *jus ad rem* (*acquirendam*), or *in personam*, it is distinguished from *jus in rem*, or proprietary right availing against all the world.

Obligations *ex contractu*, or contracts, are pacts to which legal obligations are attached.* They are I. Innominate (all made *re*), without particular names (*Do ut des*, *Facio ut facias*), and protected only by a general action, called *in factum præscriptis verbis*, which can be accommodated to any form of contract; and II. Nominate, with characteristic names and special actions attached.

I. Innominate contracts are such as *permutatio* or exchange, *precarium* or occupancy at will, *transactio* or compromise.

* For a most important account of the history of Contract, see *Ancient Law*, pp. 314-338. 1. First came the solemn *nexum*, or transaction effected *per æs et libram*, contract being at this time practically undistinguishable from mancipation or conveyance. 2. The second stage embraced the period of the four classes of nominate contracts growing up in historical order —Verbal, Literal, Real, and Consensual—when the old solemnities gradually disappeared. 3. In the last stage the prætor granted equitable actions upon Pacts or Conventions which had never been matured into contracts by *obligatio*, provided that they were based on a consideration (*causa*). These were called "Prætorian Pacts." (Cf. the History of Wills.)

II. Nominate contracts are made 1, *re;* 2, *verbis;* 3, *literis;* and 4, *consensu.* (In historical order the contracts *verbis* and *literis* come before *re*).

1. Real contracts (*re*) include all innominate contracts and four nominate: (i) *mutuum*, (ii) *commodatum*, (iii) *depositum*, and (iv) *pignus*. These contracts are completed by the mere delivery of the particular thing.

(i) *Mutuum* is a *gratuitous** loan for consumption of things which are estimated by weight, number, or measure, as metals, coin, or wine, the borrower returning not the identical things lent, but others of like nature and quantity. Such things are called *res fungibiles*, because *mutuâ vice funguntur*, and they can be replaced in kind (*in genere*).

(ii) *Commodatum* is a *gratuitous* loan of a particular thing for temporary use, to be returned in its identical form (*in specie*), as a horse or a picture. The borrower is not (as he is in *mutuum*) responsible for its loss by extraordinary accident, if he has employed the usual care of a diligent person, unless he loses it on a journey.

(iii) *Depositum* is the delivery of a thing by its owner to another to keep it *gratuitously* and to

* It is thus distinguished from a loan at interest (*fœnore*). See p. 171 n. *Nam si* MUTUAS *non potero, certum est, sumam* FŒNORE. Plautus, *Asinar.* I. 3.

restore it on demand. The depository is only answerable for *fraudulent** loss. He is said to be *in possessione* of the thing deposited, the depositor remaining both owner and *possessor* (see p. 68). A deposit (as also *pignus*) may be made *cum fiducia* for additional security. (Gai. II. 60.)

A particular kind of deposit may be made into the hands of a *sequester*, or stake-holder. *Sequester dicitur apud quem plures eandem rem, de qua controversia est, deposuerunt: dictus ab eo quod occurrenti, aut quasi sequenti eos qui contendunt, committitur.* (D. 50. 16. 110.) He is not only *in possessione*, but the actual possessor, *id enim agitur eâ depositione ut neutrius possessione id tempus procedat.* (D. 16. 3. 17.)

(iv) *Pignus* is the delivery of a thing to a creditor as a security for money due, on condition of his returning it when the debt is paid, with power of sale in default of payment. The creditor is not liable for accidental loss, but must employ the utmost care.

* *Dolus malus*, or fraud, is defined by Labeo to be *omnis calliditas, fallacia, machinatio ad circumveniendum, fallendum, decipiendum alterum adhibita.* (D. 4. 3. 1.) It vitiated every contract which it tainted.

*Culpa*, or negligence, is of two degrees: 1, *lata* (*nimia negligentia, non intelligere quod omnes intelligunt*), which was *dolo proxima;* and 2, *levissima*, or the omission of the most minute care.

*Mora* is the neglect to perform a contract within the prescribed time.

2. A verbal contract (*verbis*) is made by question and answer in the way of stipulation to give or do something, as "*Spondes?*" "*Spondeo;*" "*Promittis?*" "*Promitto;*" "*Dabis?*" "*Dabo;*" "*Facies?*" "*Faciam.*" It may be made simply or conditionally. If a particular time is fixed, the debt is due but not payable, before the expiration of the time (*cessit dies, sed nondum venit*). If the stipulation is conditional, the debt is neither due nor payable till the fulfilment of the condition, but the expectation of it may be transmitted to the heirs of the stipulator. A true condition is a future and uncertain event. Conditions relating to events which, being past or present, are certain, but uncertain as to the knowledge of the parties, either invalidate a contract, or do not delay its performance. A certain stipulation is supported by a *condictio* (p. 179), if uncertain, by an *actio ex stipulatu*. *Sicut ipsa stipulatio est, ita et intentio formulæ concipi debet.* (Gai. III. 53.)

Parties to a verbal contract are called *rei*, and may be two or more. When there are several *rei stipulandi solidum singulis debetur, et promittentes singuli in solidum tenentur; in utrâque tamen obligatione una res vertitur, et vel alter debitum accipiendo, vel alter solvendo omnium perimit obligationem et omnes liberat.* Of two joint promissors, one may contract simply, and the other conditionally, or for a particular day.

*Adstipulatores* (Gaius) are accessories to a contract on the side of the stipulator. They were originally admitted to protect his interest after death, stipulations to take effect *post mortem*, or *pridie quam moriar* or *morieris*, being invalid before Justinian: for *inelegans visum est ex heredis personâ incipere obligationem.* (Gai. III. 100.) They can adstipulate for less, but not more (either in amount or time), than their principals, and cannot transmit any right of action to their heirs. (*Vide* p. 188.)

A slave may stipulate for his master's benefit *ex personâ domini*, but cannot bind him by a promise. Neither a *peregrinus* nor his slave can stipulate under the form "*Spondes?*" which belonged exclusively to the civil law, the others being of the *jus gentium. Servus communis stipulando unicuique dominorum pro portione dominii adquirit*, unless he contracts specially in the name of one only. (Gai. III. 167.)

Stipulations are (i) judicial, proceeding from the order of a judge at the opening of a trial, as for giving security against fraud (*de dolo cautio*); (ii) prætorian, proceeding from an order of the prætor, as for giving security against anticipated injury (*damnum infectum*); (iii) conventional, made by the agreement of parties: and (iv) common, including both judicial and prætorian, as the giving security by a tutor or curator.

All property, whether movable or immovable, may be the subject of a stipulation, and *non solum res in stipulatum deduci possunt sed etiam facta, ut si stipulemur aliquid fieri vel non fieri.*

*Stipulations are invalid* on account of (i) their object, as when it does not exist, or is sacred, or religious, or when a freeman is mistaken for a slave, or the object is not owned by the giver; (ii) the persons by whom made, as when they are deaf, dumb, insane, infants (under eight), pupils (without the authority of tutor), or absent; (iii) the persons for whom made, as if one promises for another without undertaking to compel him, or stipulates for the benefit of another when he is not in the power of that other, or the latter has no interest in the performance of the promise; (iv) the persons between whom made, as between one and another in his power (this would give rise only to a natural obligation); (v) the manner, as if the answer does not agree with the question, or the stipulator contracts simply, or the promissor conditionally, or *vice versâ*, or if a man promises only some of the things stipulated for (to which alone he is bound), or if the stipulator means one thing and the promissor another; (vi) an impossible condition: *impossibilis conditio habetur cui natura impedimento est quominus existat, veluti si quis ita dixerit:* Si digito cœlum attigero, dare spondes? But if the condition be that an impossible thing shall not be done, the stipulation is valid; (vii) on account of the promise being made *ex turpi causâ.*

Justinian, changing the old law, declares that the heir of the stipulator or promissor may be sued if the condition of the stipulation is accomplished after the death of either, *ne propter nimiam subtilitatem verborum, latitudo voluntatis contrahentium impediatur.*

*Preposterous stipulations* (*i.e.* to pay *before instead of after* an event) are made valid by Justinian, *exactione post conditionem competente*—the obligation not being executed till after the fulfilment of the condition. But *nemo rem suam futuram, in eum casum quo sua sit, utiliter stipulatur.*

*Sponsores* and *fidepromissores* (Gaius) were sureties for the promissor, only in verbal contracts. They were obsolete in the time of Justinian. 1. The *Lex Apuleia* (A.U.C. 652) provided that any one who had paid more than his share might claim the excess from the rest as if co-partners. 2. The *Lex Furia* (A.U.C. 659) released them from their obligation after two years, providing that, *quotquot erunt numero eo tempore quo pecunia peti potest, in tot partes deducitur in eos obligatio, et singuli viriles partes dare jubentur;* and further *si quis solvendo non sit, non augetur onus ceterorum quotquot erunt.* (Gai. III. 121). This law applied only to Italy. 3. Their heirs were not bound (unless *peregrini fidepromissores* subject to different law). 4. A creditor was obliged to declare publicly the sum for which he took security, and the number of sureties. 5. By the *Lex Cornelia* (A.U.C. 673) no one could become surety for the same debtor to the same creditor in the same year for more than 20,000 sesterces (except in some cases, as for dower, debts under wills, or *de dolo cautio*). 6. The *Lex Publilia* gave *sponsores* a special *actio depensi in duplum* against their principals. 7. Their principals need not be legally capable of contracting, *e.g.* pupils acting without the *auctoritas* of their tutors.

*Fidejussores* are also sureties for the promissor. But, unlike the former (1), they may be added to every kind of contract, either before or after it is made. (2) They bind their heirs. (3) Where there are several, each is bound for the whole debt (*in solidum*), and the *Lex Apuleia* does not apply, but any one may claim from a magistrate (*in jure*) the *beneficium divisionis* (Hadrian), which compels the rest to share his liability. The *beneficium* is refused to those who repudiate their suretyship, and also to the *fidejussor* of a tutor. But *inter fidejussores non ipso jure dividitur obligatio ex epistolâ D. Hadriani; et ideo si quis eorum ante exactam a se partem sine herede decesserit vel ad inopiam pervenerit, pars ejus ad ceterorum onus respicit.* (D. 46. 1. 26.) This was not the case with *sponsores* and *fidepromissores*, for by the *Lex Furia* the insolvency of one did not increase the burden of the rest, and the risk of loss fell on the creditor. (4) A *fidejussor* can only be admitted when the principal is legally bound by the contract. A *fidejussor* (like an *adstipulator*, *sponsor*, or *fidepromissor*) may be bound for less, but not more, than his principal, against whom he has an *actio mandati* for money paid on his behalf. Women *fidejubere non possunt.*

In the fourth Novel Justinian gives *fidejussores* the *beneficium discussionis*, *i.e.* protection from the creditor, until the principal has been declared unable to pay the debt.

It was evidently to the advantage of the creditor to be protected by *fidejussores* rather than *sponsores* or *fidepromissores;* and this, together with the fact of their being limited to verbal contracts, will probably account for the disappearance of the latter. All three were included in the general term *adpromissores.*

3. The nominate contract, *literis*, is a written acknowledgment of debt. It was formerly created by the entry (*expensum referre*) of a *nomen* or debt, with the debtor's consent, in a ledger (*codex* or *tabulæ*) transcribed from a day-book (*adversaria*). The *nomen* was said to be *transcriptitium* (1) *a re in personam, veluti si id quod tu ex emptionis causâ mihi debeas, id expensum tibi tulero*, and (2) *a persona in personam, veluti si id quod mihi Titius debet tibi id expensum tulero, id est si Titius te delegaverit mihi.* Gaius (III. 133) says that it was a matter of much dispute whether *peregrini* were bound by this contract or not, *quia quodammodo juris civilis est talis obligatio.* The Sabinians held that in the first case (*a re in personam*) even foreigners were bound. Gaius distinguishes *nomina arcaria*, which only afford evidence of a contract made *re*. According to Theophilus, the *nomen transcriptitium* always effected a *novatio* (p. 162): *Prior obligatio extinguebatur; nova autem, id est litterarum, nascebatur.*

Unlike a verbal obligation, 1, the contract of *expensilatio* could be made in the absence of the debtor, *absenti expensum ferri potest;* 2, it could only be supported by a *condictio certi;* 3, it admitted of no conditions.

*Nomina* were obsolete in Justinian's time, but *chirographa* and *syngraphæ*, or written promises to pay, which were peculiar to *peregrini*, remained in use. Justinian allows the debtor to plead the *exceptio non numeratæ pecuniæ* (see p. 192) within two years from the date of the obligation.

4. Obligations may be formed by *mere consent* without writing, *traditio*, or the presence of the parties, in contracts of (i) *emptio-venditio*, (ii) *locatio-conductio*, (iii) *societas*, and (iv) *mandatum*. They are enforced by the prætorian* actions *empti et venditi*, *locati et conducti*, *socii*, and *mandati*.

(i) In the contract of *emptio-venditio* or sale †, a fixed money price must be *agreed on*, after which all risks and benefits connected with the thing

* The Consensual contracts were classed in the *Jus Gentium*, whence it was soon afterwards inferred that they belonged to the lost code of Nature, and to this must be attributed the support given to them by the prætors. See *Ancient Law*, pp. 332-338.

† Paul thus describes the origin of sale: *Origo emendi vendendique a permutationibus cœpit. Olim enim non ita erat nummus; neque aliud* MERX, *aliud* PRETIUM, *vocabatur. Sed unusquisque, secundum necessitatem temporum ac rerum, utilibus inutilia, permutabat, quando plerumque evenit ut quod alteri superest, alteri desit. Sed, quia non semper nec facile concurrebat ut, cum tu haberes quod ego desiderarem, invicem haberem quod tu accipere velles, electa materia est cujus publica et perpetua æstimatio difficultatibus permutationum, æqualitate quantitatis subveniret; eaque materia, formâ publicâ percussa, usum dominiumque non tam ex substantia præbet quam ex quantitate, nec ultra* MERX *utrumque, sed alterum* PRETIUM, *vocatur.* (D. 18. 1. 1 pr.)

sold attach to the purchaser, but the vendor is bound to employ due care in its preservation until delivery. *Nulla emptio sine pretio esse potest; sed et certum esse debet. Item pretium in numerata pecunia consistere debet.* Gaius says, *emptio et venditio contrahitur, cum de pretio convenerit quamvis nondum pretium numeratum sit, ac ne arra* (earnest) *quidem data fuerit.* (III. 139.) A sale may be made conditionally. In the event of the thing perishing before the happening of the condition, if the loss is total, the contract falls to the ground; if partial, the risk still attaches to the purchaser; *si exstet res, licet deterior effecta, potest dici esse damnum emptoris.* (Paul, D. 18. 6. 8.) It is void if the purchaser knowingly buys a thing *extra commercium*, as a forum or basilica. It is voidable on the ground of fraud, mistake, violence, or misrepresentation.

Being a consensual contract, sale differs from exchange, in which the obligation is formed *re*.

In the sale of a piece of land or a slave, the vendor usually undertook to pay to the purchaser double the price (*cautio duplæ*) in the event of his being dispossessed of the property bought.

The vendor need not be the proprietor of the thing sold, for he may sell a *res aliena* (cf. Legacies). The word *vendere* has thus the meaning of undertaking to furnish a thing, rather than of alienating it immediately.

(ii) The contract of *locatio-conductio*, or letting-to-hire, is, (a) of things, (b) of service. It is granted by one man to another for a certain time and at a certain price. It closely resembles sale, and the same rules apply.* *Locatio et conductio proxima est emptioni et venditioni iisdemque juris regulis consistit.* The contract is complete as soon as the *merces*, or cost of hire, is agreed on. Like the *pretium*, the *merces* must be *certa*, but it may be paid in money or in kind. Like sale, it may be made conditionally. *Jam enim non dubitatur, quin sub conditione res veniri aut locari possint.* (Gai. III. 146.) *E.g.* if a man agrees to deliver gladiators at 20 *denarii* each for the labour of those who escape unhurt, and 1000 *denarii* each for those who are killed, the first part of the contract is said to be a hiring,

* Gaius (III. 145) remarks that there are cases in which it is difficult to distinguish the two contracts: *Veluti si qua res in perpetuum locata sit, quod evenit in prædiis municipum quæ ea lege locantur, ut quamdiu id vectigal præstetur, neque ipsi conductori neque heredi ejus prædium auferatur; sed magis placuit locationem conductionemque esse.* The Emperor Zeno declared this to be a special contract, to which he gave the name of *emphyteusis* (see p. 78). The contract rested on its own agreements, but, in the absence of special arrangement, the risk of total loss fell on the proprietor, and of partial loss on the occupier. The *emphyteuta* could not be disturbed in his possession, unless he had failed to pay the *vectigal* or rent for three years.

and the second a sale. If a workman provides the materials of a thing he is employed to make, as well as the work, it is a sale and not a hiring; but if he only supplies the labour, it is a hiring. The rights and liabilities of the hirer (*conductor*) * and the *locator* pass to their heirs.

(iii) *Societas*, or partnership, is a contract by which two or more persons agree to unite their property or labour, in whole or part, equally or unequally, in a common stock, to share the profit or loss resulting therefrom. It may be for general business or for a particular transaction, and either made simply or conditionally. The shares of profit and loss are equal, unless otherwise specified. One partner may contribute money, and the other skill or labour only. A partnership in which one partner takes all the profit and the other bears all the loss (*leonina societas*) is void.

*A partnership is dissolved* by the withdrawal, death, *capitis deminutio*, or bankruptcy (*bonorum cessio*), and in the time of Gaius, *bonorum emptio* (see p. 141) of one of the partners, the confiscation of his property (*publicatio*), the completion of the transaction, or the expiration of the term for or during which it was formed.

* The *conductor* of a farm was called *colonus;* of a house, *inquilinus;* of anything to be done, *redemptor.*

But a new partnership may be contracted by mere consent; *juris enim gentium obligationes contrahere omnes homines naturali ratione possunt.* (Gai. III. 154.)

(iv) *Mandatum* (*manus datio*) or commission, is a contract by which some business is confided by one person (*mandator*) to another (*mandatarius*), who undertakes to perform it *without pay or reward.* It may be for the benefit (a) of the *mandator*, (b) of the *mandator* and *mandatarius*, (c) of a third person, (d) of the *mandator* and a third person, (e) of the *mandatarius* and a third person. A mandate for the benefit of the *mandatarius* only is of no force, nor one which is *contra bonos mores.* The *mandatarius* must not exceed the limits of the mandate. *In summa sciendum est quotiens faciendum aliquid gratis dederim, quo nomine si mercedem statuissem, locatio et conductio contraheretur, mandati esse actionem, veluti si fulloni polienda curandave vestimenta aut sarcinatori sarcienda dederim.* (Gai. III. 162.) Although the fuller or tailor would not be able to sue for any reward for his trouble by an *actio mandati*, he could employ a *cognitio extraordinaria* for that purpose. In this way the fees of advocates, doctors, and professors could be recovered.

*Mandate is extinguished* (a) by revocation before execution (*re adhuc integrâ*) by the *mandator*,

(b) by renunciation in due time by the *mandatarius*, and (c) by the death of either. If the *mandatarius* does any act in *bonâ fide* ignorance of the revocation or death of the *mandator*, it is valid. A mandate may be made conditionally, or to take effect from a particular time.

*Pacts* are simple conventions or agreements which, if founded on a consideration (*causa*) were enforced by the prætors in the later Roman jurisprudence, and hence were called Prætorian Pacts. (See *Ancient Law*, p. 377.)

II. *Quasi-contracts.* Obligations may arise *quasi ex contractu*, as well as from actual contracts.

*Quasi*-contracts are not contracts at all, because of the absence of convention, but the resemblance is strong enough to allow one to be classed as a sequel to the other, without straining the phraseology. See *Ancient Law*, p. 344. "Strictly *quasi*-contracts are acts done by one man to his own inconvenience to the *advantage* of another, but without the authority of the other, and without any promise consequently to indemnify or reward him." "*As* the party would have been obliged in case he had entered into a contract, *so* he is actually obliged by the fact which has actually happened. And as the fact which begets the obligation is, *as it were*, a convention, so is the breach of the obligation *analogous* to a breach of contract." See Austin, pp. 494, 1017, who adds that *quasi*-contracts must not be confounded with implied or tacit contracts.

1. *Negotiorum gestio*, where one person manages the affairs of another in his absence without mandate, and both are reciprocally bound. Cf. the English Salvage.

2. *Tutela* and *Curatio* (*vide* p. 56).

3. *Rei communis administratio*, where two or more persons are owners of a thing in common without partnership, and each is bound to divide the thing so possessed, and to bear his share of all proper expenses connected with it. The actions employed would be *communi dividundo*, *familiæ erciscendæ* (p. 73), or *negotiorum gestorum*.

4. *Hereditatis administratio*, or the obligation of co-heirs to divide an inheritance.

5. *Hereditatis aditio*, or the obligation of an heir who accepts an inheritance to pay the legacies charged upon it.

6. *Indebiti solutio*, or the payment by mistake *

* It is not clear whether a *condictio indebiti*, or action to recover, could be founded on a mistake of law, or only of fact. *Regula est*, says Paul, *juris quidem ignorantiam cuique nocere, facti vero ignorantiam non nocere.* D. 22. 6. 9. In the Code it is laid down that *cum quis, jus ignorans, indebitam pecuniam solverit, cessat repetitio: per ignorantiam enim facti tantum repetitionem indebiti soluti competere, tibi notum est.* C. 1. 18. 10. Papinian, however, says: *Cæterum omnibus juris error, in damnis amittendæ rei suæ, non nocet.* (D. 22. 6. 8.)

of that which is not due, in which case the recipient is bound to restore it, unless the sum paid was due in equity or by a natural obligation.*

Gaius, who does not use the division of *quasi*-contracts, says: "*Is quoque qui non debitum accepit ab eo qui per errorem solvit re obligatur. . . . Sed hæc species obligationis non videtur ex contractu consistere, quia is qui solvendi animo dat magis distrahere vult negotium quam contrahere.* (III. 91.) In the Digest, Gaius gives a third division of obligations arising *proprio quodam*

* The term "natural obligation" is used to express (1) an imperfect obligation which cannot be enforced by an action, and (2) an obligation derived from the *jus gentium* (*e.g.*, *mutuum*) as opposed to one arising from the civil law. *Naturales obligationes non eo solo æstimantur si actio aliqua earum nomine competit, verum etiam cum soluta pecunia repeti non potest.* (D. 46. 1. 16.) A natural obligation may support a plea of *compensatio* or set-off, a *fidejussio*, or a *novatio*, and it excludes the *condictio indebiti*. Only a natural obligation can arise between two persons, one of whom is in the power of the other, or between a slave and an *extraneus*, or between a debtor who has incurred a *capitis deminutio minima* and his creditor. See also *Ancient Law*, p. 335. "When a person of full intellectual maturity had deliberately bound himself by an engagement, he was said to be under a *natural obligation*, even though he had omitted some necessary formality, and even though through some technical impediment he was devoid of the formal capacity for making a valid contract." Cf. the imperfect obligations of English law, such as debts incurred by a minor, or discharged by an adjudication of bankruptcy, or barred by the Statute of Limitations.

*jure ex variis causarum figuris*, or anomalous obligations. (D. 44. 7. 1.)

Obligations, whether arising *ex contractu* or *quasi ex contractu*, may be acquired not only by a man himself but by those in his power, whether children or slaves, or by slaves of whom he has the usufruct or use, or by a freeman or a slave of another whom he possesses *bonâ fide*, when the obligation arises from something belonging to him or from the slave's labour, or by a *procurator* or agent.

*Every obligation is dissolved* by, 1, *solutio*, the unloosing of the *vinculum juris*, or satisfaction of the debt by the debtor or a third party; 2, *acceptilatio*, or imaginary payment (in verbal contracts only), when the creditor makes a solemn declaration in the form of stipulation to the debtor that he considers the debt satisfied; (by a device known as the "Aquilian stipulation," any other kind of obligation might be transformed by novation into one *ex stipulatione*, for the purpose of being discharged by acceptilation); 3, *novatio*, or the creation of a new obligation to replace an old one, (i) by a change in either of the parties, and (ii) by a change in the obligation with the same parties. Justinian provides that novation can only take place when there is an *express declaration* by the parties that they intend the old obligation to be extinguished, otherwise the new obligation merely confirms the former one. If the principal obligation is extinguished by novation, the sureties are released. Novation cannot take effect in a conditional contract, *pendente adhuc conditione.* 4, by *confusio*, when the same person becomes both debtor and creditor; 5, by *compensatio*, when one debt is set off against another; 6, by mutual consent (only in consensual contracts), if each party can be restored to his former position; 7, by the destruction of the thing due without the fault of the debtor; 8, Gaius describes an *alia species imaginariæ solutionis per æs et libram* (III. 173, 175); 9, by *litis contestatio*. (Gai. III. 180. 181.)

## 2. OF OBLIGATIONS EX DELICTO AND QUASI EX DELICTO.

Inst. IV. 1—5. Gai. III. 182—225.

A delict is a wilful offence against the law.

Delicts are, I. Public, when the offender is liable to a public accusation from any prosecutor (*vide publica judicia*, p. 198); and, II. Private, when he exposes himself to a private action at the suit only of the persons injured.*

* "The penal law of ancient communities is not the law of Crimes; it is the law of Wrongs; or, to use the English tech-

The principal private delicts are, 1, *furtum*; 2, *rapina*; 3, *damnum*; and, 4, *injuria*.

1. *Furtum* (theft) is the fraudulent taking away another's property (*contectratio rei alienæ fraudulosa*) or its use or possession for the purpose of gain. Gaius says, *Furtum autem fit non solum cum quis intercipiendi causa rem alienam amovet, sed generaliter cum quis rem alienam invito domino contrectat* (III. 195), as if a depository uses a thing left with him for his own purposes. *Interdum autem etiam liberorum hominum furtum fit, velut si quis liberorum nostrorum qui in potestate nostra sunt, sive etiam uxor quæ in manu nostra sit, subreptus fuerit.* (III. 199.) It is, (i) *manifestum*, if the thief is taken in the act, or with the thing stolen on him before he has reached his destination (penalty four times the value); and otherwise, (ii) *nec manifestum* (penalty double the value).

In the *old* law *furtum* was called, 1, *conceptum*, when a thing stolen was found before witnesses

nical word, of Torts. The person injured proceeds against the wrong-doer by an ordinary civil action, and recovers compensation in the shape of money-damages, if he succeeds." "Offences which we are accustomed to regard exclusively as *crimes* are exclusively treated as *torts*, and not theft only, but assault and violent robbery are associated by the juris-consult with trespass, libel, and slander. All alike give rise to an obligation or *vinculum juris*, and were all requited by a payment of money." *Ancient Law*, p. 370.

in a man's house, though he might not have been the thief (also in case of solemn search, *lance licioque conceptum*); 2, *oblatum*, when it was transferred to another person by the thief from fear of discovery, and then seized in his house, such transferee having an *actio oblati* against the thief; 3, *prohibitum*, when a person was prevented from searching for a thing stolen; 4, *non exhibitum*, when a person did not produce a thing stolen that had been searched for and found in his possession. The actions *furti concepti* and *oblati* were for treble the value, *prohibiti* and *non exhibiti* for quadruple. (All these distinctions had disappeared in the time of Justinian.)

No theft can be committed without intent to steal. But *sola cogitatio furti faciendi non facit furem.* (D. 47. 2. 1.)

A man may steal his own property, as if a debtor takes from a creditor that which he has pledged to him.

A confederate (*ope, consilio*) in a theft is liable to an *actio furti*, as if one knocks money from a man's hand that another may seize it, or scatters a flock of sheep or herd of oxen that another may steal some of them; *et hoc veteres scripserunt de eo qui panno rubro fugavit armentum.* (Gai. III. 202.)

A person who receives and conceals stolen goods is liable to an *actio furti nec manifesti*.

*Abigeatus* is the offence of cattle-lifting. *Abigei habentur qui pecora ex pascuis, vel ex armentis subtrahunt, et quodammodo deprædantur, et abigendi studium quasi artem exercent, equos de gregibus, vel boves de armentis abducentes. Abigeatus crimen publici judicii non est: quia furtum magis est. Oves pro numero abactorum aut furem aut abigeum faciunt. Quidam decem oves gregem esse putaverunt; porcus etiam quinque, vel quatuor abactos; equum, bovem vel unum abigeatus crimen facere.* (D. 47. 14.)

There is no right of action for theft between a parent or master, and those in his power.

An *actio furti* may be brought by a person interested in the safety of the thing stolen, though he is not the owner. But the thing must have been delivered to him, and a bailee cannot bring an action unless he is solvent, but must leave it to the owner to recover. *E.g.*, if clothes are sent to a tailor and then stolen, the *actio furti* belongs to the tailor (if solvent) and not to the owner, who has an *actio locati* against the tailor, but if the tailor is insolvent the owner has the action for theft.

If a borrower has the property borrowed stolen, the owner has the choice of an *actio commodati* against the borrower, or an *actio furti* against the thief, but he cannot bring both.

If a thing given in pledge is stolen, the creditor and not the debtor has the *actio furti*.

If a thing stolen is possessed by a *bonâ fide* purchaser, he has the *actio furti*.

A depository cannot bring an action for theft, not being responsible for loss, but the owner may.

By the law of the XII Tables, the penalty for *furtum manifestum* was *capitalis*, *i.e.*, affecting not necessarily the life, but the *caput* (p. 55) of the individual. A free person was flogged and assigned over as a bondsman to the man he had robbed: a slave suffered flogging and death. The prætor substituted the *actio quadrupli*. (See Gai. III. 189—194, and *Ancient Law*, p. 378.)

The *actio furti* aims only at recovering the penalty (quadruple or double the value), but the owner may recover the thing itself by a *vindicatio*, or an *actio ad exhibendum* against any possessor, or by a *condictio furtiva*, which reaches not only the thief but his heirs.

2. *Rapina* (robbery) is the theft of property committed with violence. The robber is said to be an *improbus fur* (an unconscionable thief): *quis enim magis alienam rem invito domino contrectat quam qui rapit?* (Gai. III. 209.)

The *actio vi bonorum raptorum*, if brought within

a year, enables the owner to recover (as in *furtum manifestum*) fourfold restitution (*i.e.*, the thing itself, and three times its value); but after a year, only the thing or its single value. Like the *actio furti*, it may be brought by almost any person having an interest in the property stolen, though he is not the owner. The constitutions extended the action to the case of forcible entrance on immovable property.

3. *Damnum* is the damage or loss sustained by the wrongful destruction or injuring of property.

*The Aquilian law* was passed to establish an action (*legis Aquiliæ*, or *damni injuriâ*) to give redress for *damnum injuria factum*. It provides, 1, that if any person kills wrongfully the slave or beast* of another, he shall pay the owner the highest market value for which such slave or beast could have been sold during the previous year. This does not apply to killing without fault, or in self-defence. But a physician is liable for want of skill, so also a careless driver or rider. In taking the value of the thing destroyed, all further loss arising from its destruction must be calculated, *e.g.*, if one of four horses forming a

* Those animals only are included *quæ pecudum numero sint*, and the law does not apply to wild beasts and dogs. But Gaius says that elephants and camels come under the provision, because *quasi mixti sunt: nam et jumentorum operam præstant, et natura eorum fera est.* (D. 9. 2. 2.)

team or *quadriga* is killed, *id quoque computatur quanti depretiati sunt qui supersunt.* 2. An action is given against an adstipulator, who, to defraud the stipulator, has released the promissor from his debt by acceptilation. Gai. III. 215. (Obsolete in time of Justinian.) 3. If a person inflicts any kind of damage on any kind of property, whether animate or inanimate, without killing man or beast, he is liable to pay the owner the highest market value that such property possessed during the previous thirty days.

A direct action under the Aquilian law can only be brought against one who has caused the injury with his own body (*corpore corpus læsum*). Otherwise a *utilis* (from the adverb *uti*), or analogous, *actio* is given;* *e.g.*, against one who has persuaded another man's slave to climb a tree, or go down a well, to his injury.

4. *Injuria* is an outrage to the person or character by something said or done with malicious intent (*dolo malo*). (It is also used generally to mean *omne quod non jure fit.*) See Gai. III. 220-222.

By the law of the XII Tables, the penalty was

* The *utilis actio* was given by the prætor to supply any defect in the *directa actio*, or to enlarge or mitigate the ancient civil law. (See Austin, Lect. 35, p. 621.) There were thus two kinds of *actiones utiles*, (1) in which the civil law was not noticed at all, and (2) in which it was ostensibly relied on, but extended by a fiction to a case not properly within it. (Lindley's *Jurisprudence.*)

simple retaliation (*talio*) for limb or member destroyed, but for a broken bone, 300 *asses* in the case of a free person, and 150 for a slave. (Gai. III. 223.)

The prætorian law allows the person injured to recover damages calculated according to his rank, and the nature and circumstances of the injury. The action extends to cases in which a man has been injured in the person of those in his power, or of his wife, though not *in manu*, and it reaches those who have assisted in the injury by word or deed. No injury can be done to a slave, but only through him to his master or co-masters, if it be *atrox*.

The *Lex Cornelia* also provides a civil action for violent injuries, as beating or maltreating a person, or forcibly entering his house, the damages to be assessed by the judge. The violator is also liable to a criminal prosecution.

An *injuria* is said to be *atrox*, or aggravated, by reason of its nature, the place where it is committed, or the rank of the person injured.

*The action for injury is extinguished*, 1, by death; 2, the delay of a year; 3, remission; 4, satisfaction.

*Quasi-delicts.* Obligations may arise from *quasi-delicts*,* or circumstances analogous to delicts, as

* *Quasi-delict* is "an incident by which *damage* is done to

from the wrong decision of a judge who has "made a suit his own," and become liable for damage (p. 198), or when things have been thrown or poured from a house, or placed in a dangerous position, or where property has been lost or stolen in a ship or an inn, the master being liable.

Gaius does not notice *quasi*-delicts in the Commentaries, but he says in the Digest, *Judex non proprie ex maleficio obligatus videtur; sed quia neque ex contractu, obligatus est, et utique peccasse aliquid intelligitur, licet per imprudentiam, ideo videtur quasi ex maleficio teneri in factum actione, et in quantum de eâ re æquum religioni judicantis visum fuerit, pœnam sustinebit.* (D. 50. 13. 6.)

the obligee (though without the negligence or intention of the obligor), and for which damage the obligor is bound to make satisfaction. It is not a delict because intention or negligence is of the essence of a delict." Austin, p. 945.

The XII Tables limited the rate of interest to *unciarium fœnus*, or an annual payment (in the old year of ten months) of one twelfth of the sum lent (*sors*), which equals the modern 10 per cent. Nieb. *Rom. Hist.* III. 61. Later, the *sors* was divided into hundredths, and the highest legal interest was fixed at $\frac{1}{100}$ (*centesima, legitima, usura*), or one per cent. per month, payable on the 1st (Kalends), *i.e.* 12 per cent. a year. This did not extend to *fœnus nauticum* (D. 22. 2. 1.), or *pecunia trajectitia* (money advanced on maritime adventures), on which the rate was unlimited till Justinian fixed the *maximum* at 12, and on ordinary loans, at 6 per cent. C. 4. 32. 26. 1. See Heinec. p. 534.

# BOOK IV.—OF ACTIONS.

## SYSTEMS OF PROCEDURE IN CIVIL ACTIONS.

### Inst. IV. 6—14. Gai. IV. 1—129.

I. *Legis Actiones.*
1. *Sacramenti* (applying in most cases).
2. *Judicis postulatio* (in actions *de finibus, de tutelâ,* &c.)
3. *Condictio* (for definite thing or sum).
4. *Manus injectio.* } Modes of execution.
5. *Pignoris capio.* } Modes of execution.

The ancient *legis actiones* are described by Gaius (IV. 11—31). They were eminently Quiritary, and could only be employed between Roman citizens. The prætorian or equitable actions had not yet been introduced.

The issue was decided (*in judicio*) with solemn but almost pantomimic forms by *judices** or *arbitri* appointed by a magistrate (*in jure*) to try the case after he had directed them as to the law. The *judex* was sworn to decide *ex animi sententia et ex lege.* Like the English juror, he was a simple citizen, and his duties ended with the termination of the case. At first only persons of

* *Pedanei judices* (*hoc est, qui negotia humiliora disceptant,* C. 3. 3. 5) were so called because they sat *non in tribunali, ut magistratus, sed in subselliis, veluti ad pedes Prætoris.* Heinec. p. 737.

senatorial rank were chosen for the office, but the other classes were gradually admitted. A list of selected *judices* was publicly drawn up by the prætor. *Arbitri* were those who had before them the *arbitrium et facultatem totius rei* (Festus). Proceedings could only take place on the *dies fasti* (see p. 121) which were determined by the *pontifices*. The functions of the *prætor* or magistrate were expressed by the three words *dare, dicere, addicere, i.e.*, (1) to grant an action and appoint a *judex*, (2) to declare the rule of law applying to the case, and (3) to ascribe the contested right to the successful party.

There were also permanent tribunals which consisted successively of (1) the college of *pontifices*, (2) the *Decemviri*, and (3) the *Centumviri*. From the time of the great jurists the *Centumviri* dealt only with questions of succession.

The *legis actiones*, however, gradually fell into discredit from the excessive nicety of their technicalities. *Sed istæ omnes legis actiones paulatim in odium venerunt, namque ex nimia subtilitate veterum qui tunc jura condiderunt eo res perducta est, ut vel qui minimum errasset litem perderet.* (Gai. IV. 30.) Accordingly they were chiefly suppressed by the *Lex Æbutia* (B.C. 180), and almost entirely by the *Leges Juliæ* of Augustus. (See Appendix, p. 203.)

II. The system of *formulæ* which were composed of the . . .
1. *Demonstratio* (statement of facts and ground of action).
2. *Intentio* (plaintiff's claim).
3. *Condemnatio* (giving the *judices* the right to condemn or absolve the defendant).
4. *Adjudicatio* (giving them the power to adjudicate).

See Gaius, IV. 39—44, 130—137.

*Formulæ* were *conceptæ*, 1, *in jus*, to try questions of law; 2, *in factum*, to try questions of fact; and 3, both *in jus* and *in factum*. (See Gai. IV. 45—52.)

The formulary system probably originated in the necessity of providing judicial decisions on cases arising between *cives* and *peregrini*. The *prætor peregrinus* was first appointed in 246 B.C., he and the *prætor urbanus* holding interchangeable offices. The judges to whom he referred disputes were called *recuperatores*. They always sat in the number of three, four, or five together, while a *judex* often tried a case alone. In the time of Gaius there were eighteen prætors at Rome, and the Curule Ædiles had a considerable share in the administration of civil justice.* In the other towns of Italy the jurisdiction belonged to the *duumviri* or prefects; in the provinces, generally to the governor.

* *Judicia* were (1) *legitima* and (2) *imperio continentia*, or *quæ imperio magistratus continentur*. The former were tried before only one *judex*, and either in Rome or within a mile of the city.

1. The first step was the *in jus vocatio*, or summons. If the defendant undertook to appear on another day, he had to enter into a *vadimonium* or engagement, with or without sureties (*satisdatio*). 2. When the parties had appeared in court the plaintiff declared his form of action (*editio actionis*), and applied to the magistrate for a *formula* (*actionis postulatio*). 3. If the defendant could not successfully resist the granting of an action on any grounds, the magistrate appointed a *judex*, and drew up a *formula* determining the questions to be decided. The delivery of the *formula*, *cum judicium accipitur*, was the moment of the *litis contestatio* (cf. joinder-of-issue), which ended the proceedings *in jure*. *Lis tunc contestata videtur quum judex per narrationem negotii causam audire cœperit.* (C. 3. 9. 1.) It also extinguished the plaintiff's right of action on the same ground. *Bis de eadem re agi non potest.* (Gai. III. 180, 181.) 4. The parties then appeared *in judicio*, produced witnesses, argued the case, and received the decision of the *judex* (interlocutory or final); but the old ceremonies were dispensed with. (See Inst. IV. 17. *De officio judicis.*) The case might

The latter were cases in which *peregrini* were concerned, or which were heard beyond a mile from Rome. They were so called because they only lasted as long as the prætor who granted them retained his *imperium*. See Gai. *IV. 103—109.*

also be decided in the absence of the defendant. 5. For execution it was necessary to apply again to the magistrate. 6. The colleague of the magistrate, or his superior, or a tribune of the people, might stay execution (*intercedere*) to allow an appeal to a higher court. An appeal would lie from the decision of a *judex* to the magistrate who appointed him, or to the emperor.

In some few cases (as in the summary *restitutio in integrum* and the *missio in bonorum possessionem*) the prætor united the offices of magistrate and *judex*. Interdicts flourished during this period, which lasted till A.D. 342, when all the *formulæ* were abolished by Constantius II.: *Juris formulæ aucupatione syllabaram insidiantes cunctorum actibus, radicitus amputentur.* (C. 2. 58. 1.)

Gaius (IV. 31—38) mentions some of the fictions employed in pleading under the formulary system through the operation of *utiles actiones* (p. 169): *e.g.*, a *bonorum possessor* or *emptor* averred that he was the heir, *ficto se herede* (Rutilian and Servian actions). *Item civitas Romana peregrino fingitur. Præterea aliquando fingimus adversarium nostrum capite deminutum non esse.* "The object of these *fictiones* was of course to give jurisdiction, and they therefore strongly resembled the allegations in the writs of the English Queen's

Bench and Exchequer, by which those courts contrived to usurp the jurisdiction of the Common Pleas:—the allegation that the defendant was in custody of the king's marshal, or that the plaintiff was the king's debtor, and could not pay his debt by reason of the defendant's default." See *Ancient Law*, pp. 25—28.

Gaius also mentions *præscriptiones* (IV. 130—137), so called from being prefixed to the *formulæ*, which might be added by the plaintiff to limit the demand made in the *intentio*, if too large, or (before the time of Gaius) by the defendant to raise some preliminary question.

III. *Extraordinaria Judicia.* Under this system the trial by *judices* was abolished, their functions being merged in those of the magistrate. This process alone existed in the time of Justinian. *Extra ordinem jus dicitur qualia sunt hodie omnia judicia.* (Inst. IV. 15.)

At Rome and Constantinople justice was administered by the prefect of the town and the *prætor urbanus.* In the other towns by the municipal magistrates, generally called *defensores.* In the provinces the ordinary jurisdiction belonged to the governors (*præsides, proconsules, rectores*) with assessors, an appeal being allowed to the rulers of each prefecture, who severally represented the emperor.

In this procedure the plaintiff's claim or bill was called a *libellus conventionis*, which was answered by *exceptiones.*

An action is (1) the power of having recourse to a public authority to redress a grievance, (2) the process or suit itself so employed. Celsus defines it as the *jus persequendi in judicio quod sibi debetur*. (D. 44. 7. 51.)

I. Actions are, 1, real (*in rem*); 2, personal (*in personam*); and 3, mixed.

1. A real action (*rei vindicatio*, or *petitio*) is brought to establish a claim to the property of a thing itself, whether corporeal or incorporeal, as against all the world, being founded on *dominium* or *jus in rem.*

Gaius says that under the formulary system *in rem actio duplex est: aut enim per formulam petitoriam agitur, aut per sponsionem.* (Gai. IV. 91.) By the *formula petitoria* the plaintiff claimed the property as his own. By the *sponsio* a sort of wager was entered into called a *stipulatio pro præde litis et vindiciarum*, as a preliminary proceeding with a view to obtaining a decision on the case. *Ideo autem appellata est quia in locum prædium* (sureties) *successit*. (See Gai. IV. 92—94.)

An *actio confessoria* is an action *in rem* brought by one who claims a right of servitude, whether prædial or personal. It may be brought against the owner of the property, or any one who impedes the exercise of the right.

An *actio negativa* is brought by one who claims that his property is not burdened with a servitude. It is not employed *in controversis rerum corporalium.*

2. A personal action is brought to recover something due from a particular person, *ex contractu* or *ex delicto,* being founded on *obligatio,* or *jus ad rem* (*acquirendam**). See p. 144.

Besides *condictiones,* or actions by which *dare fierive oportere intendimus* (Gai. IV. 5), there are many other personal actions, as those *bonæ fidei, vi furti,* and *legis Aquiliæ.* In the language of the old law *condictio* was equivalent to *denuntiatio* or notice to the defendant to present himself at the end of thirty days to receive a *judex.* (See Gai. IV. 18.)

3. A mixed action seeks to recover both a specific thing and the performance of a personal obligation, as (i) *familiæ erciscendæ,* (ii) *communi dividundo,* and (iii) *finium regundorum* (*vide* p. 73).

II. In their origin actions are, 1, civil, or derived from the civil law (*ex legitimis et civilibus causis*), and 2, prætorian, from the *jus honorarium.*

The prætorian law allows many actions forbidden by the rigour of the civil law; *e.g.*, I. of

* An expression invented in the Middle Ages.

real actions, 1, *actio Publiciana*, giving a remedy to a purchaser who has lost property delivered to him by one who (though the *bonâ fide* possessor) is not the *dominus* and cannot pass the *dominium*; or (formerly) to whom a *res mancipi* had been transferred by the *dominus* by simple delivery instead of *mancipatio* (such a purchaser is said to be *in causâ usucapiendi*, but the action is allowed also in the case of things which are not susceptible of usucapion, see p. 80); 2, *actio rescissoria*, to recover property lost through absence abroad by the usucapion of another, on the ground that the prescription is not complete; 3, *actio Pauliana*, by which creditors may recover goods fraudulently alienated by the debtor; 4, *actio Serviana*, given to the owner of a farm to recover from any possessor goods pledged by the tenant to secure his rent; 5, *actio quasi-Serviana*, for the recovery of things pledged or hypothecated to creditors; 6, *actiones prœjudiciales* (preliminary proceedings to ascertain facts), (i) *de libertate*, (ii) *de ingenuitate*, (iii) *de partu agnoscendo*. Gaius speaks of other *actiones prœjudiciales* (IV. 44), as to discover *quanta dos sit*, or whether a creditor who takes *sponsores* or *fidepromissores* has declared publicly the amount of his debt and the number of his sureties (p. 151). II. Of personal actions, 1, *actio de constituta pecunia*, to enforce a mere promise or agreement *pro se vel pro alio* without stipulation (by the old law a plaintiff in this action could claim in addition one half of the orginal sum, Gai. IV. 171); 2, *de peculio*, to compel a father or master to perform the contract of his son or slave to the extent of their *peculium;* 3, *de jurejurando*, to inquire whether a person has made oath that a sum is due. III. *Ex delicto.* Justinian, following Gaius (IV. 46), says that the penal actions established by the prætor are innumerable. He gives the three following instances: 1, *de albo corrupto*, against one who has damaged the prætor's tablet; 2, *de in jus vocando*, against one who has summoned his father or patron without leave from the prætor; and 3, *de in jus vocato vi exempto,* against one who has forcibly or fraudulently prevented the appearance of a person summoned before the prætor. In *depositum necessarium*, *i.e.*, made *tumultûs*, *incendii*, *ruinæ*, *naufragii causâ*, the prætor allows an *actio dupli* against the depository, or against his heir, if personally guilty of fraud.

When a delict has been committed by more than one person, a penal action is always given *in solidum* against each delinquent.

III. With regard to their object, actions are, 1, for the thing itself *in rem persecutoriæ;* 2, for a penalty; and 3, for both, as in the *actio vi bonorum raptorum* (*vide* p. 167); or for delay in payment of a legacy bequeathed to a sacred place.

IV. Actions are for the single, double, treble, or quadruple value, beyond which no action extends. The thing itself or its single value is sued for in cases of *stipulatio*, *mutuum*, *mandatum*, *&c.*; the double value in *furtum nec manifestum*, *damnum injuria ex lege Aquiliâ*, the corruption of a slave, &c.; the treble value when a plaintiff (*actor*) claims more than is due to him (*plus-petitio*, p. 183); the quadruple value in *furtum manifestum*, *quod metus causâ* (contracts induced by intimidation), or in case of corruption in instituting or desisting from a suit.

V. Actions again are (according to the powers of the judge), 1, *bonæ fidei;* 2, *stricti juris;* and 3, *arbitrariæ*.

1. Actions *bonæ fidei* are all prætorian, considerations being admitted (according to rules of equity) of (i) *dolus malus*, (ii) custom, (iii) *compensatio*, or set off; and (iv) interest is allowed on debts overdue. Such are actions *empti et venditi*, *mandati*, *commodati*, *&c.*

2. In actions *stricti juris* the judge is bound by the letter of the civil law, as in the *actiones ex stipulatu* and *ex testamento*.

3. In *actiones arbitrariæ* (both real and personal)

the judge has discretionary powers to award damages or compensation on principles of equity according to the special circumstances of the case: *e.g.*, in the *actiones Serviana* and *ad exhibendum*. *Arbitraria actio utriusque utilitatem continet tam actoris quam rei: quod si rei interest, minoris fit pecuniæ condemnatio quam intentatum est; aut si actoris majoris fit.* (D. 13. 4. 2 pr.)

Gaius says, *omnium autem formularum quæ condemnationem habent ad pecuniariam æstimationem condemnatiò concepta est. Itaque etsi corpus aliquod petamus, velut fundum, hominem, vestem, aurum, argentum, judex non ipsam rem condemnat eum cum quo actum est, sicut olim fieri fiebat, sed æstimata re pecuniam eum condemnat.* (IV. 48.)

A certain or uncertain thing may be the subject of an action.

A plaintiff may correct a mistake in his claim in the same action.

A *plus-petitio* may be made (i) *re*, (ii) *tempore*, (iii) *loco*, (iv) *causâ*. Under the formulary system *si quis agens in intentione suâ plus complexus fuerit quam ad eum pertineret, causâ cadebat, id est rem amittebat.* By the law of Justinian (founded on a constitution of Zeno) if a *plus-petitio* is made *tempore*, the time which remains between the day of claim and the day of payment is doubled. Thus, if a debt is due in three months from the time of claim, the debtor gains three extra months. In all other kinds of *plus-petitio* the plaintiff is liable to pay treble the amount of the defendant's loss. If the plaintiff demands less than his due, the judge may condemn the defendant to pay the balance. There can, of course, be no *plus-petitio* in a claim for an uncertain amount.

VI. Actions may be for the whole or part of a debt: *e.g.*, in a claim against the *peculium* of a son or slave, where the father is only liable to the extent of the *peculium*, or in an *actio de dote* (to recover dower), where the husband is liable only to the extent of his means (*beneficium competentiæ*), all necessary expenses of the *dos* being allowed.

By the old law the husband was allowed to retain part of the dower for certain causes (see p. 86). The *retentiones* were, however, suppressed by Justinian. He could also bring an action against his wife *propter res donatas, propter res amotas*, and *de moribus*. (Gai. IV. 102.) Formerly, on the dissolution of marriage, a woman had two actions for the recovery of her *dos*, viz., *rei uxoriæ* and *ex stipulatu*. The latter could arise only from a formal stipulation, but it was the more advantageous form, because being an *actio stricti juris* it admitted of no delay or deductions in the restitution of the *dos*. Justinian abolishes the action *rei uxoriæ*, allowing in all cases the action *ex stipulatu* which he makes *bonæ fidei.* The husband thus gains the *beneficium competentiæ* and a year's delay for restoring *res dotales* except immovables, which he must give up immediately. The action is given equally whether the *dos* is *adventitia* or *profectitia*, and whether the marriage is dissolved by the death of the husband or the wife.

The *beneficium competentiæ* is also allowed in an action against an ascendant or patron by his descendant or freedman, or against a partner or donor by his partner or donee, or (formerly) against a debtor by a creditor, to whom he had made a *cessio bonorum*, for property since acquired. (See p. 141). A soldier who has contracted debts is never condemned for more than *quatenus facere potest.* (D. 42. 1. 6 pr.)

A defendant may claim the right of set-off. *Compensatio*, says Modestinus, *est debiti et crediti inter se contributio.* (D. 16. 2. 1.) *Ideo compensatio necessaria est, quia interest nostrâ potius non solvere quam solutum repetere.* (Pomponius, D. 16. 2. 3.) Gaius explains the difference between *compensatio* and *deductio* (IV. 66—69). *Nostra constitutio*, says Justinian, *eas compensationes quæ jure aperto nituntur, latius introduxit; ut actiones ipso jure minuant sive in rem, sive in personam, sive alias quascunque; exceptâ solâ depositi actione, cui ali-*

*quid compensationis nomine opponi satis impium esse credidimus, ne, sub prætextu compensationis, depositarum rerum quis exactione defraudetur.* (Inst. IV. 6. 30.)

VII. Actions are, 1, *directæ*, when brought against a person for his own act; 2, *indirectæ*, for the act of those in his power.

A parent or master is liable for the contracts of those in his power, 1, if he has ordered them; 2, if he has profited by them. The plaintiff may proceed by a prætorian action or a *condictio.* The prætor gives the following actions: 1, *quod jussu*, to those who have contracted with a son or slave, by order of his father or master, for the performance of such contract by the father or master; 2, *exercitoria*,* against a shipowner who has contracted through his servants in command of his ship; 3, *institoria*,† against a principal who has contracted through his factors or brokers; 4, *tributoria*, to the creditors of a son or slave who has traded

* *Quicunque in societate navali, suo periculo naves vel fluminibus, vel mari ipsi, immittebant, sive suas, sive per aversionem conductas, ii* EXERCITORES *vocabantur. Unde exercitor est, ad quem obventiones omnes et reditus navis perveniunt, sive is dominus navis sit, sive a domino per aversionem conduxerit.*

† *Non facile solebant mercatores magnarii ipsi in tabernis versari, sed vel servos, vel libertos, vel liberos homines, mercede conductos negotiationibus præficere, quos* INSTITORES *adpellabant eo, quod negotio gerendo instarent.* Heinec. p. 695.

with his *peculium* with the consent of his father or master to compel the profits to be distributed between the creditors and the father or master; 5, *de peculio* (*vide* p. 181); 6, *de in rem verso,* to recover what a father or master has converted to his own profit out of the contract of his son or slave as far as the amount of the profits will extend.

*SC Macedonianum.** In the case of money lent to children under power without the consent of the father, this *SC* forbids any action against the father or children, even when the latter have become *sui juris.*

VIII. Actions are, 1, perpetual; and 2, temporary.

Formerly actions derived from the law, *SCC,* or constitutions, were perpetual, but a limit of thirty or forty years was afterwards assigned by a constitution of Theodosius II. (A.D. 424).

Of prætorian actions some are *perpetuæ* (thirty or forty years) as those given to *bonorum possessores,* and the *actio furti manifesti,* but the greater part only last for one year, the period of a prætor's office.

* So called either from one Macedo, a notorious usurer, or from a profligate son of that name, who, being under power, had borrowed money which he expected to repay on the death of his father. *Multo tempore elapso, instabat creditor debitum repetens: Macedo non habens unde redderet (quî enim, cum sub potestate esset?) patrem suum occidit.* (Theophilus.)

IX. Most actions *ex contractu* pass to and against the heirs of the parties, but some do not, as the *actio in duplum* for money deposited to insure against fire or shipwreck, and actions arising from adstipulations (see p. 148).

Actions *ex delicto* cannot be brought against the heirs of the delinquent (though they pass to those of the person injured) unless the proceedings have been begun by the original parties, or the heir has profited by the misdeeds of the deceased. *Est certissima juris regula, ex maleficiis pœnales actiones in heredem non competere.* (Gai. IV. 112.)

X. *Noxal* Actions.* When damage is done by a slave, the master is liable to a noxal action, but he may elect to abandon the slave to the person injured before the *litis contestatio.* But he cannot escape a penalty if he has falsely denied his possession of the slave (D. 2. 9. 2), or if he has not prevented the offence when it was in his power to do so. (D. 9. 4. 2 pr.) The action follows the wrongdoer if he changes hands. *Noxalis actio caput sequitur.* No action is allowed between master and slave. The person to whom the slave is abandoned (whose property he becomes) is

* Noxal is derived from *Nocere.* *Noxa* is strictly the author of the damage, *noxia* the delict itself, but they are sometimes used synonymously.

bound to enfranchise him if he can promise a sufficient sum to compensate for the damage done.

By the old law, a son or daughter under power could be abandoned *noxaliter*, but this rule had disappeared in Justinian's time. *Nova hominum conversatio* (referred by some to Christianity) *hujusmodi asperitatem recte respuendam esse existimavit, et ab usu communi hæc penitus recessit.* (Inst. IV. 8. 7.)

*Pauperies.* Damage done by a domesticated quadruped without *injuria* (for an animal cannot be said to have wrong intent) renders the owner liable to a noxal action, but not if the animal is fierce by nature. Alfenus gives the following example: — *Agaso* (a groom) *cum in tabernam equum deduceret, mulam equus olfecit; mula calcem rejecit, et crus agasoni fregit. Consulebatur, possetne cum domino mulæ agi, quod ea pauperiem fecisset? Respondi, posse.* (D. 9. 1. 5.) An *actio utilis* is given in the case of animals other than quadrupeds. The action is stayed by delivering up the animal. If an animal which has been kept in confinement recovers its natural liberty, the person to whom it belonged ceases to be the owner, and is no longer liable for injury. If a man keeps a dog, a pig, a wild boar, a lion, or a bear near a highway, he is liable to an action under the edict of the ædiles for damage done by such animal, as well as to a noxal action, *nunquam enim actiones, præsertim pœnales, de eâdem re concurrentes, alia aliam consumit.*

*Representatives in Actions.* In the time of the old *legis actiones*, no one could represent another in an action, except on behalf, 1, of the people (*pro populo*); 2, of a slave to be emancipated (*pro libertate*); 3, of a pupil (*pro tutelâ*); and, 4, an *actio furti* could be brought in the name of persons in the hands of an enemy, or absent in the service of the State. In the time of the *formulæ*, *cognitores*, *procuratores*, and *defensores* were admitted to appear for principals. The *cognitor* was solemnly appointed in the presence of the magistrate and of the opposite party, and his principal was bound by his acts. He could not be appointed conditionally. The *procurator* was appointed without any solemnity, and his acts did not affect his principal unless ratified by him. Later, under the *extraordinaria judicia*, the *procurator* was vested with the authority of the *cognitor*, whose name fell into disuse. The *defensor* appeared (generally only for the defendant) without any appointment. Tutors and curators could also appear for their pupils and wards.

*Security. Satisdationum modus alius antiquitati placuit, alium novitas per usum amplexa est.* (Inst. IV. 11 pr.) By the *old* law a defendant in a real action appearing in person or by another had to give security *judicatum solvi*, which guaranteed, 1, that the damages would be paid, 2, that he would appear in court to receive sentence (*judicatum sisti*), 3, that he would not employ fraud (*de dolo malo*). Appearing in person in a personal action a defendant had no security to give, except in certain cases, *propter genus actionis* (as *de moribus mulieris*), or *propter personam, quia suspecta sit* (as if he is a bankrupt): if he pleaded through another, he was bound *satisdare*, for *nemo defensor in alienâ re sine satisdatione idoneus esse creditur*. The plaintiff in a real or personal action only had to give security in case he appeared by a *procurator* that he would confirm his acts (*rem ratam dominum habiturum* or *de rato*). For further details, see Gai. IV. 101, 102.

By the law of Justinian the plaintiff in a real or personal action has only to give the security *de rato* when he acts as *procurator absentis* not publicly appointed. The defendant appearing in person, even in a real action, only has to give security *judicatum sisti*. But when represented by a *procurator* or *defensor*, the *cautio judicatum solvi* must be given. He must also find a *fidejussor*, or surety (if present he may be his own surety), and give a *hypotheca* or mortgage of his property binding his heirs.

*Exceptiones.* The defence to an action is made by exceptions. *Comparatæ sunt exceptiones defendendorum eorum gratia cum quibus agitur: sæpe enim accidit, ut quis jure civili teneatur, sed iniquum sit eum judicio condemnari.* (Gai. IV. 116.) Originally they were restrictions imposed on the decision of a judge by the prætor from considerations of equity (*si in eâ re nihil dolo malo factum sit, neque fiat*). They were afterwards adopted by the civil law.

They are addressed, (i), *in jus*, to dispute a question of law, (ii), *in factum*, to try a question of fact. They are also (i), *in rem*, affecting the general matter in dispute, and (ii), *in personam*, touching the personal liability of the defendant.

Exceptions are either, 1, perpetual and peremptory, or 2, temporary and dilatory.

1. Perpetual and peremptory exceptions repel the plaintiff's case on its merits, and destroy for ever his right of action; *e.g.*, *doli mali*, *metus causâ*, *pecuniæ non numeratæ* (where one has stipulated to pay money but has not paid it), and *rei judicatæ* (that the cause has been already decided).

Gaius mentions also the *exceptio rei in judicium deductæ*, which may be made by one of two joint promissors when each has been separately sued. (III. 181, and IV. 106, 107.)

2. Temporary and dilatory exceptions are framed

to delay an action which is essentially just, but brought at a wrong time or in an improper manner; *e.g.*, *pacti conventi* (where the plaintiff has agreed not to sue within a certain time), and *litis dividuæ* (where a plaintiff splits his action for a single thing into two), also (before Justinian) objections to a *procurator*.

Most of the exceptions allowed to a debtor are available also to his sureties.

*Nuda pactio* (p. 143) *non parit obligationem, sed parit exceptionem.* (D. 2. 14. 7.)

*Replications.* The plaintiff may make a *replicatio* to the exceptions, and the defendant may answer again by a *duplicatio*, to which the plaintiff has the right of a *triplicatio*. The pleadings may be extended still further.

Theodosius II.

## OF INTERDICTS.

Inst. IV. 15. Gai. IV. 138—170.

Under the formulary system, interdicts were certain forms of words by which the prætor ordered or forbade something to be done, generally in disputes as to possession or *quasi*-possession of property.

Justinian abolishes them, supplying their place with actions in the *judicia extraordinaria.*

They were, 1, prohibitory (as to prevent an act of violence); 2, restoratory (to place the rightful owner in possession, though for the first time); 3, exhibitory (ordering some person or thing to be exhibited).

They were generally given that possession might be (i) acquired (*adipiscendæ possessionis*); (ii) retained (*retinendæ*); (iii) recovered (*recuperandæ*).

(i) Of those for acquiring possession were (1) *quorum bonorum,* to compel the delivery to the *bonorum possessor* of goods belonging to an inheritance. 2. *Bonorum quoque emptori similiter proponitur interdictum quod quidam possessorium vocant.* 3. *Item ei qui publica bona emerit, ejusdem conditionis interdictum proponitur quod appellatur sectorium, quod sectores vocantur qui publicè bona mercantur*. (Gai. IV. 145, 146.) 4. The *interdictum Salvianum* to enforce the right of an owner of land to the property of his tenant pledged as security for rent (*cf. actio Serviana*, p. 180).

(ii) Of those for retaining possession were, (1) *uti possidetis*, given to one who was in possession of land or buildings (acquired *nec vi nec clam nec precario*), that he might be declared to be the legal possessor; (2) *utrubi*, given for the same purpose to one who had been in possession of movable property (acquired *nec vi nec clam nec precario*) for the greater part of the previous year.

Gaius explains these two interdicts (IV. 150-2). Justinian says that the actions which superseded them are both placed on the same footing as regards possession, whether the property be movable or immovable. (Inst. IV. 15.)

A man may retain possession by anyone who possesses in his name; *e.g.*, a tenant, or depository, or borrower, and even by the mere intention of possessing. *Possidere videmur, non solum si ipsi possideamus, sed etiam si nostro nomine aliquis in possessione sit, licet si nostro juri subjectus non sit, qualis est colonus et inquilinus* (p. 157 n.) *Per eos quoque apud quos deposuerimus, aut quibus commodaverimus, aut quibus usufructum vel usum aut gratuitam habitationem constituerimus, ipsi possidere videmur; et hoc est quod vulgo dicitur, retineri posses-*

*sionem posse per quemlibet qui nostro nomine sit in possessione.* (Gai. IV. 153.)

(iii) The principal interdict for recovering possession was called *unde vi*, given to one who had been expelled by force from possession of land or buildings. Afterwards extended to movable property.

The principal interdicts given to establish *quasi*-possession (as servitudes) were *uti possidetis*, *utrubi*, *unde vi*, or specially, *de itinere actuque privato*, *de fonte*, &c.

Interdicts were also, 1, simple, where one party was plaintiff and the other defendant, as in restitutory or exhibitory interdicts; and 2, double, where each party equally sustained the character of plaintiff and defendant, as in *uti possidetis* and *utrubi*.

Cattle-lifting (Abigeatus), p. 166.

## OF GROUNDLESS LITIGATION AND OF THE OFFICE OF JUDGE.

Inst. IV. 16, 17. Gai. IV. 171—187.

Under the old law there were four modes of repressing vexatious suits. *Actoris calumnia coercetur, modo calumniæ judicio, modo contrario* (cross-action), *modo jurejurando, modo restipulatione.* (Gai. IV. 174.) By the law of Justinian groundless proceedings at law are restrained, 1, by a *pecuniaria pœna;* 2, by oath; and 3, by fear of infamy.

1. A plaintiff who fails in an action must pay the costs of the defendant. *Victus victori in impensis damnandus est.* Children or freedmen who summon (*vocant in jus*) their ascendants or patrons without leave from the prætor are liable to a fine of 50 *solidi.* 2. The plaintiff and defendant and their respective advocates must make oath that they believe they have a good case. 3. Infamy is incurred by persons condemned in direct actions *tutelæ, mandati, depositi,* and *pro socio,* and in actions *furti, vi bonorum raptorum, injuriarum,* and *de dolo.* A person branded with infamy cannot serve as a witness, be admitted to honours, or bring a public accusation.

*The duty of a judge* is to decide according to

the laws, the constitutions, and customs. In the actions *familiæ erciscendæ, communi dividundo,* and *finium regundorum,* he has to adjudicate according to the rights of the parties. If he gives an unjust decision by mistake of law, or through fraud, corruption, or ignorance, or goes beyond the scope of the case, he is said to "make a cause his own," and is liable to an action from the injured person for damages. In case of a mistake of fact, the decision is good, subject to appeal. A *judex* may divest himself of his office by swearing *sibi non liquere.*

## OF PUBLICA JUDICIA.

### Inst. IV. 18.

Public prosecutions are employed for the punishment of criminals, and are open to every citizen. They are not introduced by actions. *Publica judicia neque per actiones ordinantur neque omnino quidquam simile habent cum cæteris judiciis de quibus locuti sumus, magnaque diversitas est eorum et in instituendis et in exercendis.* (Inst. IV. 18. pr.)

They are, 1, capital (*i.e.*, affecting the *caput* of the criminal, p. 55) involving death, *interdictio aquæ et ignis, deportatio,* or sentence to the mines; and 2, not capital, involving infamy and pecuniary penalties.*

* "The classifications of crimes, which are not contained even

The *Lex Julia Majestatis* punishes treason with death, coupled with perpetual infamy. See Paul, *Sent. Rec.* V. 29.

The *Lex Julia de Adulteriis* punishes adultery with death, and seduction *sine vi* with confiscation of half the fortune in the case of the rich, and corporal punishment and relegation in the case of the poorer classes.

The *Lex Cornelia de Sicariis* condemns assassins to death. See Paul, *Sent. Rec.* V. 23.

The *Lex Pompeia de Parricidiis* provides that those guilty of the murder of a parent, grand-parent, or child, shall be sewn up in a leather sack with a dog, a cock, a viper, and a monkey, and thrown into sea or river, that the air may be denied them while they survive, and the earth

in the Corpus Juris of Justinian, are remarkably capricious." "The Statutes of Sylla and Augustus were the foundation of the penal jurisprudence of the Empire, and nothing can be more extraordinary than some of the classifications which they bequeathed to it. I need only give a single example in the fact that *perjury* was always classed with *cutting* and *wounding*, and with *poisoning*, no doubt because a law of Sylla, the Lex Cornelia de Sicariis et Veneficis, had given jurisdiction over all these three forms of crimes to the same Permanent Commission. It seems, too, that this capricious grouping of crimes affected the vernacular speech of the Romans. People naturally fell into the habit of designating all the offences enumerated in one law by the first name on the list, which doubtless gave its style to the law court deputed to try them." *Ancient Law*, p. 393. See also p. 385 for an account of the History of Criminal Law.

when they are dead. *Hodie tamen vivi exuruntur, vel ad bestias dantur.* (Paul, *Sent. Rec.* V. 24).

The *Lex Cornelia de Falsis* punishes the forging or fraudulently tampering with wills and other instruments. A slave suffers death, a freeman *deportatio.* See Paul, *Sent. Rec.* V. 25.

The *Lex Julia de Vi Publica seu Privata* punishes public violence with *deportatio*, and private violence with confiscation of one-third of the offender's property. Rape is punished with death. See Paul, *Sent. Rec.* V. 26.

The *Lex Julia de Peculatu* punishes robbery of public or sacred property with *deportatio*, but in the case of magistrates, with death.

The *Lex Fabia de Plagiariis* punishes with fine (sometimes with death) those guilty of *plagium*, or the fraudulent imprisonment, sale, abduction, or concealment of a free citizen, or another man's slave.

The *Lex Julia de Ambitu* prohibits unlawful means of obtaining public office, or dignity.

The *Lex Julia Repetundarum* punishes magistrates or judges for bribery and corruption.

The *Lex Julia de Annonâ* prohibits combinations for raising the market prices of provisions.

The *Lex Julia de Residuis* punishes embezzlement or maladministration of public moneys.

"The Institutes close with a short title, 'De

Publicis Judiciis,' which only includes a *species* of Criminal Procedure, together with the Crimes and Punishments to which that species was appropriate. It would seem that this title in the Institutes is not a member or constituent part of the work, but rather a hasty and incongruous appendix added on an afterthought. For, first, instead of expounding the subject in a systematic manner, it merely touches a *fragment* of the subject. Secondly, it appears that Criminal Law was looked upon by the Roman Jurists as properly forming a department of Jus Publicum; and *this*, it is most probable, was not included in the Treatises from which Justinian's Institutes were copied or compiled. Whether a similar title was appended to the Institutes of Gaius is uncertain, the concluding portion of the manuscript being lost or illegible." Austin, Tables and Notes, p. 959.

The brevity of the notice of Criminal Law is explained in the concluding passage of the Institutes: *Sed de publicis judiciis hoc exposuimus, ut vobis possibile sit summo digito et quasi per indicem ea tetigisse: alioquin diligentior eorum scientia vobis ex latioribus Digestorum libris, Deo propitio, adventura est.*

# CONTENTS OF THE APPENDIX.

# APPENDIX.

*From* "GIBBON'S ROMAN EMPIRE," *Chap.* XLIV.

*Forms of the old Roman Law.*—"The jurisprudence of the first Romans exhibited the scenes of a pantomime; the words were adapted to the gestures, and the slightest error or neglect in the *forms* of proceeding was sufficient to annul the *substance* of the fairest claim. The communion of the marriage-life was denoted by the necessary elements of fire and water; and the divorced wife resigned the bunch of keys by the delivery of which she had been invested with the government of the family. The manumission of a son or a slave was performed by turning him round with a gentle blow on the cheek; a work was prohibited by the casting of a stone; prescription was interrupted by the breaking of a branch; the clenched fist was the symbol of a pledge or deposit; the right hand was the gift of faith and confidence. . . . . In a civil action, the plaintiff touched the ear of his witness, seized his reluctant adversary by the neck, and implored, in solemn lamentation, the aid of his fellow-citizens. The two competitors grasped each other's hand, as if they stood prepared for combat before the tribunal of the prætor; he commanded them to produce the object of the dispute; they went, they returned with measured steps, and a clod of earth was cast at his feet to represent the field for which they contended.

This occult science of the words and actions of law was the inheritance of the pontiffs and patricians. . . . The treachery of some plebeian officers at length revealed the profitable mystery; in a more enlightened age the legal actions were derided and observed, and the same antiquity which sanctified the practice, obliterated the use and meaning of this primitive language."

*Reforms of Justinian.*—"When Justinian ascended the throne, the Reformation of the Roman jurisprudence was an arduous but indispensable task. In the space of ten centuries the infinite variety of laws and legal opinions had filled many thousand volumes, which no fortune could purchase and no capacity could digest. Books could not easily be found; and the judges, poor in the midst of riches, were reduced to the exercise of their illiterate discretion. The subjects of the Greek provinces were ignorant of the language that disposed of their lives and properties; and the *barbarous* dialect of the Latins was imperfectly studied in the academies of Berytus and Constantinople. As an Illyrian soldier, that idiom was familiar to the infancy of Justinian; his youth had been instructed in the lessons of jurisprudence, and his Imperial choice selected the most learned civilians of the East to labour with their sovereign in the work of reformation. . . . . As soon as the Emperor had approved their labours, he ratified, by his legislative power, the speculations of the jurisconsults: their commentaries on the Twelve Tables, the Perpetual Edict, the laws of the people, and the decrees of the senate, succeeded to the authority of the text; and the text was abandoned, as an useless, though venerable, relic of antiquity. The

*Code*, the *Pandects*, and the *Institutes*, were declared to be the legitimate system of civil jurisprudence; they alone were admitted in the tribunals, and they alone were taught in the academies of Rome, Constantinople, and Berytus. Justinian addressed to the Senate and provinces his *eternal oracles;* and his pride, under the mask of piety, ascribed the consummation of this great design to the support and inspiration of the Deity."

*The paternal power.*—"In the forum, the senate, or the camp, the adult son of a Roman citizen enjoyed the public and private rights of a *person;* in his father's house he was a mere *thing;* confounded by the laws with the moveables, the cattle, and the slaves, whom the capricious master might alienate or destroy without being responsible to any earthly tribunal. The hand which bestowed the daily sustenance might resume the voluntary gift, and whatever was acquired by the labour or fortune of the son was immediately lost in the property of the father. His stolen goods (his oxen or his children) might be recovered by the same action of theft; and if either had been guilty of a trespass, it was in his own option to compensate the damage, or resign to the injured party the obnoxious animal. At the call of indigence or avarice, the master of a family could dispose of his children or his slaves. . . . . According to his discretion, a father might chastise the real or imaginary faults of his children by stripes, by imprisonment, by exile, by sending them to the country to work in chains among the meanest of his servants. The majesty of a parent was armed with the power of life and death; and the examples of such bloody executions, which were sometimes praised and never punished, may be traced in the annals of Rome, beyond the times of Pompey and Augustus. Neither age, nor rank, nor the consular office, nor the honours of a triumph, could exempt the most illustrious citizen from the bonds of filial subjection: his own descendants were included in the family of their common ancestor; and the claims of adoption were not less sacred or less rigorous than those of nature. . . . An imperfect right of property was at length communicated to sons; and the threefold distinction of *profectitious*, *adventitious*, and *professional*, was ascertained by the jurisprudence of the Code and Pandects. Of all that proceeded from the father he imparted only the use, and reserved the absolute dominion; yet, if his goods were sold, the filial portion was excepted, by a favourable interpretation, from the demands of the creditors. In whatever accrued by marriage, gift, or collateral succession, the property was secured to the son; but the father, unless he had been specially excluded, enjoyed the usufruct during his life. As a just and prudent reward of military virtue, the spoils of the enemy were acquired, possessed, and bequeathed by the soldier alone; and the fair analogy was extended to the emoluments of any liberal profession, the salary of public service, and the sacred liberality of the emperor or the empress. The life of a citizen was less exposed than his fortune to the abuse of paternal power. . . The Roman father, from the licence of servile dominion, was reduced to the gravity and moderation of a judge. . . . . A private jurisdiction is repugnant to the spirit of monarchy; the parent was again reduced from a judge to an accuser; and the magistrates were enjoined by Severus Alexander to hear his complaints and execute his sentence. He could no longer take the life of a son without incurring the guilt and punishment of murder; and the pains of parricide, from which he had been excepted by the Pompeian law, were finally inflicted by the justice of Constantine."

*Marriage.*—"Experience has proved that savages are the tyrants of the female sex, and that the condition of women is usually softened by the refinements of social life. In the hope of a robust progeny, Lycurgus had delayed the season of marriage: it was fixed by Numa at the tender age of twelve years, that the Roman husband might educate to his will a pure and obedient virgin. According to the custom of antiquity, he bought his bride of her parents, and she fulfilled the *coemption* by purchasing, with three pieces of copper, a just introduction to his house and household duties. A sacrifice of fruits was offered by the pontiffs in the presence of ten witnesses; the contracting parties were seated on the same sheepskin; they tasted a salt cake of *far*, or rice; and this *confarreation*, which denoted the ancient food of Italy, served as an emblem of their mystic union of mind and body. But this union on the side of the woman was rigorous and unequal, and she renounced the name and worship of her father's house to embrace a new servitude, decorated only by the title of adoption: a fiction of the law, neither rational nor elegant, bestowed on the mother of a family (her proper appellation) the strange characters of sister to her own children and of daughter to her husband or master, who was invested with the plenitude of paternal power. By his judgment or caprice her behaviour was approved, or censured, or chastised; he exercised the jurisdiction of life and death; and it was allowed that in the cases of adultery or drunkenness the sentence might be properly inflicted. She acquired and inherited for the sole benefit of her lord; and so clearly was woman defined, not as a *person*, but as a *thing*, that, if the original title were deficient, she might be claimed, like other moveables, by the *use* and possession of an entire year.

"After the Punic triumphs the matrons of Rome aspired to the common benefits of a free and opulent republic; their wishes were gratified by the indulgence of fathers and lovers, and their ambition was unsuccessfully resisted by the gravity of Cato the Censor. They declined the solemnities of the old nuptials, defeated the annual prescription by an absence of three days, and, without losing their name or independence, subscribed the liberal and definite terms of a marriage contract. Of their private fortunes, they communicated the use and secured the property: the estates of a wife could neither be alienated nor mortgaged by a prodigal husband; their mutual gifts were prohibited by the jealousy of the laws; and the misconduct of either party might afford, under another name, a future subject for an action of theft. To this loose and voluntary compact religious and civil rights were no longer essential, and between persons of a similar rank the apparent community of life was allowed as sufficient evidence of their nuptials. The dignity of marriage was restored by the Christians, who derived all spiritual grace from the prayers of the faithful and the benediction of the priest or bishop. The origin, validity, and duties of the holy institution, were regulated by the tradition of the synagogue, the precepts of the Gospel, and the canons of general or provincial synods; and the conscience of the Christians was awed by the decrees and censures of their ecclesiastical rulers. Yet the magistrates of Justinian were not subject to the authority of the church: the emperor consulted the unbelieving civilians of antiquity; and the choice of matrimonial laws in the Code and Pandects is directed by the earthly motives of justice, policy, and the natural freedom of both sexes."

*The right of property.*—"The original right of property can only be justified by the accident or merit of prior occupancy; and on this foundation it is wisely established by the philosophy of the civilians. The savage who hollows a tree, inserts a sharp stone into a wooden handle, or applies a string to an elastic branch, becomes in a state of nature the just proprietor of the canoe, the bow, or the hatchet. The materials were common to all; the new form, the produce of his time and simple industry, belongs solely to himself. His hungry brethren cannot, without a sense of their own injustice, extort from the hunter the game of the forest overtaken or slain by his personal strength and dexterity. If his provident care preserves and multiplies the tame animals, whose nature is tractable to the arts of education, he acquires a perpetual title to the use and service of their numerous progeny, which derives its existence from him alone. If he encloses and cultivates a field for their sustenance and his own, a barren waste is converted into a fertile soil; the seed, the manure, the labour, create a new value, and the rewards of harvest are painfully earned by the fatigues of the revolving year. In the successive states of society, the hunter, the shepherd, the husbandman, may defend their possessions by two reasons which forcibly appeal to the feelings of the human mind: that whatever they enjoy is the fruit of their own industry; and that every man who envies their felicity may purchase similar acquisitions by the exercise of similar diligence. Such, in truth, may be the freedom and plenty of a small colony cast on a fruitful island. But the colony multiplies, while the space continues the same; the common rights, the equal inheritance of mankind, are engrossed by the bold and crafty: each field and forest is circumscribed by the landmarks of a jealous master; and it is the peculiar praise of the Roman jurisprudence that it asserts the claim of the first occupant to the wild animals of the earth, the air, and the waters. In the progress from primitive equity to final injustice, the steps are silent, the shades are almost imperceptible, and the absolute monopoly is guarded by positive laws and artificial reason. The active, insatiate principle of self-love can alone supply the arts of life and the wages of industry; and as soon as civil government and exclusive property have been introduced, they become necessary to the existence of the human race. . . . . A Roman citizen could only forfeit his rights by apparent dereliction, and such dereliction of a valuable interest could not easily be presumed. Yet, according to the Twelve Tables, a prescription of one year for moveables and of two years for immoveables, abolished the claim of the ancient master, if the actual possessor had acquired them by a fair transaction from the person whom he believed to be the lawful proprietor. Such conscientious injustice, without any mixture of fraud or force, could seldom injure the members of a small republic; but the various periods of three, of ten, or of twenty years, determined by Justinian, are more suitable to the latitude of a great empire."

*Hereditary succession.*—"The personal title of the first proprietor must be determined by his death; but the possession, without any appearance of change, is peaceably continued in his children, the associates of his toil, and the partners of his wealth. This natural inheritance has been protected by the legislators of every clime and age, and the father is encouraged to persevere in slow and distant improvements, by the tender hope that a long posterity will enjoy the fruits of his labour. The *principle* of hereditary succession is universal; but the *order* has been variously established by convenience or caprice, by the spirit of national institutions, or by some partial example which was originally decided by fraud or violence. The jurisprudence of the Romans appears to have deviated from the equality of nature much less than the Jewish, the Athenian, or the English institutions. On the death of a citizen, all his descendants, unless they were already freed from his paternal power, were called to the inheritance of his possessions. The insolent prerogative of primogeniture was unknown; the two sexes were placed on a just level; all the sons and daughters were entitled to an equal portion of the patrimonial estate; and if any of the sons had been intercepted by a premature death, his person was represented, and his share was divided, by his surviving children. On the failure of the direct line, the right of succession must diverge to the collateral branches. The degrees of kindred are numbered by the civilians, ascending from the last possessor to a common parent, and descending from the common parent to the next heir: my father stands in the first degree, my brother in the second, his children in the third, and the remainder of the series may be conceived by fancy or pictured in a genealogical table. In this computation a distinction was made, essential to the laws and even the constitution of Rome: the *agnats*, or persons connected by a line of males, were called, as they stood in the nearest degree, to an equal partition; but a female was incapable of transmitting any legal claims; and the *cognats* of every rank, without excepting the dear relation of a mother and a son, were disinherited by the Twelve Tables, as strangers and aliens. Among the Romans a *gens* or lineage was united by a common *name* and domestic rites; the various *cognomens* or *surnames* of Scipio or Marcellus distinguished from each other the subordinate branches or families of the Cornelian or Claudian race: the default of the *agnats* of the same surname was supplied by the larger denomination of *gentiles;* and the vigilance of the laws maintained, in the same name, the perpetual descent of religion and property. A similar principle dictated the Voconian law, which abolished the right of female inheritance. As long as virgins were given or sold in marriage, the adoption of the wife extinguished the hopes of the daughter. But the equal succession of independent matrons supported their pride and luxury, and might transport into a foreign house the riches of their fathers. While the maxims of Cato were revered, they tended to perpetuate in each family a just and virtuous mediocrity; till female blandishments insensibly triumphed, and every salutary restraint was lost in the dissolute greatness of the republic. The rigour of the decemvirs was tempered by the equity of the prætors. Their edicts restored emancipated and posthumous children to the rights of nature; and upon the failure of the *agnats*, they preferred the blood of the *cognats* to the name of *gentiles*, whose title and character was insensibly covered with oblivion. The reciprocal inheritance of mothers and sons was established in the Tertullian and Orphitian decrees by the humanity of the senate. A new and more impartial order was introduced by the Novels of Justinian, who affected to revive the jurisprudence of the Twelve Tables. The lines of masculine and female kindred were confounded: the descending, ascending, and collateral series, was accurately defined; and each degree, according to the proximity of blood and affection, succeeded to the vacant possessions of a Roman citizen."

*Wills.*—"Before the time of the decemvirs, a Roman citizen exposed his wishes and motives to the assembly of the thirty curiæ or parishes, and the general law of inheritance was suspended by an occasional act of the legislature. After the permission of the decemvirs, each private lawgiver promulgated his verbal or written testament in the presence of five citizens, who represented the five classes of the Roman people; a sixth witness attested their concurrence; a seventh weighed the copper money, which was paid by an imaginary purchaser, and the estate was emancipated by a fictitious sale and immediate release. This singular ceremony, which excited the wonder of the Greeks, was still practised in the age of Severus ; but the prætors had already approved a more simple testament, for which they required the seals and signatures of seven witnesses, free from all legal exception, and purposely summoned for the execution of that important act. A domestic monarch, who reigned over the lives and fortunes of his children, might distribute their respective shares according to the degrees of their merit or his affection ; his arbitrary displeasure chastised an unworthy son by the loss of his inheritance, and the mortifying preference of a stranger. But the experience of unnatural parents recommended some limitations of their testamentary powers. A son, or, by the laws of Justinian, even a daughter, could no longer be disinherited by their silence : they were compelled to name the criminal and to specify the offence ; and the justice of the emperor enumerated the sole causes that could justify such a violation of the first principles of nature and society. Unless a legitimate portion, a fourth part, had been reserved for the children, they were entitled to institute an action or complaint of *inofficious* testament—to suppose that their father's understanding was impaired by sickness or age, and respectfully to appeal from his rigorous sentence to the deliberate wisdom of the magistrate."

*Legacies.*—" In the Roman jurisprudence an essential distinction was admitted between the inheritance and the legacies. The heirs who succeeded to the entire unity, or to any of the twelve fractions of the substance of the testator, represented his civil and religious character, asserted his rights, fulfilled his obligations, and discharged the gifts of friendship or liberality which his last will had bequeathed under the name of legacies. But as the imprudence or prodigality of a dying man might exhaust the inheritance, and leave only risk and labour to his successor, he was empowered to retain the *Falcidian* portion; to deduct, before the payment of the legacies, a clear fourth for his own emolument. A reasonable time was allowed to examine the proportion between the debts and the estate, to decide whether he should accept or refuse the testament; and if he used the benefit of an inventory, the demands of the creditors could not exceed the valuation of the effects. The last will of a citizen might be altered during his life, or rescinded after his death: the persons whom he named might die before him, or reject the inheritance, or be exposed to some legal disqualification. In the contemplation of these events, he was permitted to substitute second and third heirs to replace each other according to the order of the testament; and the incapacity of a madman or an infant to bequeath his property might be supplied by a similar substitution. But the power of the testator expired with the acceptance of the testament: each Roman of mature age and discretion acquired the absolute dominion of his inheritance, and the simplicity of the civil law was never clouded by the long and intricate entails which confine the happiness and freedom of unborn generations."

*Codicils and trusts.*—"Conquest and the formalities of law established the use of *codicils*. If a Roman was surprised by death in a remote province of the empire, he addressed a short epistle to his legitimate or testamentary heir, who fulfilled with honour, or neglected with impunity, this last request, which the judges before the age of Augustus were not authorised to enforce. A codicil might be expressed in any mode or in any language, but the subscription of five witnesses must declare that it was the genuine composition of the author. His intention, however laudable, was sometimes illegal, and the invention of *fideicommissa*, or trusts, arose from the struggle between natural justice and positive jurisprudence. A stranger of Greece or Africa might be the friend or benefactor of a childless Roman, but none, except a fellow-citizen, could act as his heir. The Voconian law, which abolished female succession, restrained the legacy or inheritance of a woman to a sum of one hundred thousand sesterces; and an only daughter was condemned almost as an alien in her father's house. The zeal of friendship and parental affection suggested a liberal artifice: a qualified citizen was named in the testament, with a prayer or injunction that he would restore the inheritance to the person for whom it was truly intended. Various was the conduct of the trustees in this painful situation; they had sworn to observe the laws of their country, but honour prompted them to violate their oath; and if they preferred their interest under the mask of patriotism, they forfeited the esteem of every virtuous mind. The declaration of Augustus relieved their doubts, gave a legal sanction to confidential testaments and codicils, and gently unravelled the forms and restraints of the republican jurisprudence. But as the new practice of trusts degenerated into some abuse, the trustee was enabled, by the Trebellian and Pegasian decrees, te reserve one-fourth of the estate, or to transfer on the head of the real heir all the debts and actions of the succession. The interpretation of testaments was strict and literal; but the language of *trusts* and codicils was delivered from the minute and technical accuracy of the civilians."

*Abuses of civil jurisprudence.*—"The penal statutes form a very small proportion of the sixty-two books of the Code and Pandects, and in all judicial proceeding the life, or death of a citizen is determined with less caution and delay than the most ordinary question of covenant or inheritance. This singular distinction, though something may be allowed for the urgent necessity of defending the peace of society, is derived from the nature of criminal and civil jurisprudence. Our duties to the state are simple and uniform; the law by which he is condemned is inscribed not only on brass or marble, but on the conscience of the offender, and his guilt is commonly proved by the testimony of a single fact. But our relations to each other are various and infinite; our obligations are created, annulled, and modified by injuries, benefits, and promises; and the interpretation of voluntary contracts and testaments, which are often dictated by fraud or ignorance, affords a long and laborious exercise to the sagacity of the judge. The business of life is multiplied by the extent of commerce and dominion, and the residence of the parties in the distant provinces of an empire is productive of doubt, delay, and inevitable appeals from the local to the supreme magistrate. Justinian, the Greek emperor of Constantinople and the

East, was the legal successor of the Latian shepherd who had planted a colony on the banks of the Tiber. In a period of thirteen hundred years the laws had reluctantly followed the changes of government and manners; and the laudable desire of conciliating ancient names with recent institutions destroyed the harmony and swelled the magnitude of the obscure and irregular system. The laws which excuse on any occasions the ignorance of their subjects, confess their own imperfections; the civil jurisprudence, as it was abridged by Justinian, still continued a mysterious science and a profitable trade, and the innate perplexity of the study was involved in tenfold darkness by the private industry of the practitioners. The expense of the pursuit sometimes exceeded the value of the prize, and the fairest rights were abandoned by the poverty or prudence of the claimants. . . . The experience of an abuse from which our own age and country are not perfectly exempt may sometimes provoke a generous indignation, and extort the hasty wish of exchanging our elaborate jurisprudence for the simple and summary decrees of a Turkish cadhi. Our calmer reflection will suggest that such forms and delays are necessary to guard the person and property of the citizen; that the discretion of the judge is the first engine of tyranny; and that the laws of a free people should foresee and determine every question that may probably arise in the exercise of power and the transactions of industry. But the government of Justinian united the evils of liberty and servitude, and the Romans were oppressed at the same time by the multiplicity of their laws and the arbitrary will of their master."

Printed in Dunstable, United Kingdom

91221349R00130